"This is a beautifully w
heart and lead you throu
of balance and peace – eve.., ...

Sue Johnson, (EdD), *Founder of Emotionally Focused Therapy & Director of the International Centre for Excellence in Emotionally Focused Therapy (ICEEFT)*

"Who hasn't felt the crushing pain of heartache after a relationship breakup? Whether you are in the throes of a fresh heartbreak or are perseverating about an old flame who was "the one that got away", this book will be a beacon of guidance and support. What Dr Rosoman offers is a roadmap that helps people heal emotionally from a lost love and rebuild their lives. She brings her many years of clinical experience as a psychologist and relationship therapist to help readers gain self-awareness and insight about what makes relationships last."

Veronica Kallos-Lilly, (Ph.D.), *ICEEFT Certified Trainer in Emotionally Focused Therapy; co-author of* An Emotionally Focused Workbook for Couples: The Two of Us *2nd edition (Routledge, 2022)*

"Clare has written something extraordinary here. Since people are realizing that time doesn't heal all wounds, many are seeking and needing relevant, accessible assistance that is rooted in science without being overly scientific. Clare has written such a book. It is warm and friendly but clear and actionable. Clare has applied attachment science to the experience of heartbreak in a way that is very leading edge. This book provides excellent, well written, accessible information provided in bite-sized, digestible pieces. There is a process ahead for those of us grieving, and as she highlights at the beginning, she remains with the reader throughout! It is an excellent and most relevant resource and would have been my best companion in my own dark hours of grief. I have benefitted from reading it and I can't wait until I can give it as a gift, recommend it to clients, and share it with my loved ones!"

Kathryn Rheem, (EdD), *Trainer in Emotionally Focused Therapy; Director of the Washington Baltimore Center for EFT, & Co-Founder of the EFT Café*

An Emotionally Focused Guide to Relationship Loss

By viewing romantic love as an attachment bond, Clare Rosoman incorporates emotionally focused therapy (EFT) and attachment theory to provide evidence-based tools in navigating close relationships and managing the pain of relationship loss.

Beginning with a foreword from Veronica Kallos-Lilly, this book firstly explores how attachment themes show up in relationship dynamics, creating either security or insecurity, before looking at how relationships go wrong. Chapters then focus on creating a new narrative for this loss of connection, helping readers learn about their own attachment strategies and how to work through pain, anger, and grief. The last part focuses on helping readers learn how to forgive, let go, build security within themselves, and implement these strategies in future relationships.

Addressing all forms of relationships, including family and friendship losses, LGBTQ+ couples, and references to cultural humility, this accessible and empathetic guide is written for both therapists and their clients to help them learn from their experiences and build the ability to be a resource for themselves. It is essential reading for EFT therapists as well as couple, marriage, and family therapists.

Clare Rosoman is a clinical psychologist, and EFT therapist and trainer based in Queensland, Australia.

An Emotionally Focused Guide to Relationship Loss

Life After Love

Clare Rosoman

Routledge
Taylor & Francis Group

NEW YORK AND LONDON

Cover image: Cover photograph by Clare Rosoman

First published 2022
by Routledge
605 Third Avenue, New York, NY 10158

and by Routledge
4 Park Square, Milton Park, Abingdon, Oxon, OX14 4RN

Routledge is an imprint of the Taylor & Francis Group, an informa business

© 2022 Clare Rosoman

Library of Congress Cataloging-in-Publication Data
A catalog record for this title has been requested

ISBN: 978-1-032-20562-5 (hbk)
ISBN: 978-1-032-20561-8 (pbk)
ISBN: 978-1-003-26416-3 (ebk)

DOI: 10.4324/9781003264163

Typeset in Sabon
by KnowledgeWorks Global Ltd.

Dedication
To my husband Nicholas and my children James and Sophie for being my safe haven and secure base.

Contents

Foreword by Veronica Kallos-Lilly

Who hasn't felt the crushing pain of heartache after a relationship breakup? Whether you are in the throes of a fresh heartbreak or are perseverating about an old flame who was "the one that got away," this book will be a beacon of guidance and support. What Dr. Rosoman offers is a roadmap that helps people heal emotionally from a lost love and rebuild their lives. She brings her many years of clinical experience as a psychologist and relationship therapist to help readers gain self-awareness and insight about what makes relationships last.

There are plenty of books out there that recycle old cliches about getting through breakups. What is fresh about Life After Love is that it gets to the root of relationship breakdown and helps the reader reflect astutely on their own role in the creation of an insecure bond. You will learn about your own patterns in relationships, your emotional reactions and behaviours when you are not feeling secure, and how you might inadvertently trigger insecurity in a partner, resulting in distressing interactions. Based on Emotionally Focused Therapy (EFT), the gold standard in treating relationships, this book goes into depth about the emotions typically experienced as part of grieving a lost love. It not only illuminates how to work through the "big" emotions of hurt, anxiety, anger, sadness, despair, guilt, etc., but also how to regulate their intensity and glean the wisdom inherent in them.

Dr. Rosoman draws upon decades of research on emotion and relationship bonding that she sprinkles throughout the book, along with rich case examples of clients that help illuminate what you are learning. Insightful reflective questions will structure and deepen your understanding of yourself. The "takeaways" section helps crystallise the key points at the end of each chapter and provide an easy reference to go back to and consolidate your learning.

Thus, this book not only supports readers in navigating the healing process, but it also helps you rebuild and sets you up to better shape security in future relationships. The author accomplishes these goals in highly accessible and practical ways, striking a seamless balance between learning, reflecting, and integrating. What struck me most in reading this book, however, was the incredible care and compassion Dr. Rosoman conveys through the written word. Throughout this book, you will be accompanied by the voice of an incredibly wise and deeply empathic therapist who is guiding your growth based on a solid foundation of attachment theory and research on close relationships. If you want to come away understanding how your relationship deteriorated and developing the capacity to build strong and secure relationships in the future, you will be most thankful you picked up this book!

Veronica Kallos-Lilly, Ph.D.
ICEEFT Certified EFT Therapist, Supervisor and Trainer
Co-author of *An Emotionally Focused Workbook for Couples:*
The Two of Us

Acknowledgements

I owe a debt of gratitude to my wonderful parents who gave me a secure start in life. What a gift that is.

I want to acknowledge Professor Susan Johnson for her contribution to the adult attachment literature and for her pioneering work in developing Emotionally Focused Therapy (EFT). She has literally changed the face of relationship therapy. I am grateful to have learned from her and been inspired by her in doing the work that I do to improve relationships. I have been mentored by some wonderful attachment-based EFT master-therapists along my journey and want to express my thanks to them for their guidance and support in helping me to grow in so many ways, both personally and professionally. Dr. Veronica Kallos-Lilly, Dr. Kathryn Rheem, and Dr. Jennifer Fitzgerald, you have all been and remain to be so important to me as a source of solace and inspiration.

I want to acknowledge the collective wisdom of the special people who let me see into their hearts and share in their love when they enter my therapy space. This book is an assembly of my learnings built over time, enabled by the openness and generosity of the wonderful humans I have been lucky enough to walk beside. It is my hope that this might be a vehicle to share their wisdom, so that it might help others.

Introduction

Let's start this book with an honest confession: I am a hopeless romantic. I am wholeheartedly in the business of keeping relationships together. As a relationship therapist, I invest a *whole* lot into other people finding and maintaining love relationships, to repairing them when they go wrong, to growing together and championing each other. All in the service of the "happy-ever-after" situation. I contort myself into all kinds of pretzel shapes to help people to stay together and to find lasting love. As I said, I am indeed a hopeless romantic.

So, in creating a book about surviving the loss of a relationship, this is a bizarre place to find myself. I am a Clinical Psychologist who, for the majority of my career, has worked mostly with people struggling both with themselves and with their relationships. I am an avid believer in the healing potential of secure bonds with those who matter most to us. I have devoted my professional study to the literature on attachment theory (as discussed later) and have studied and learned about the best attachment-based therapies such as Emotionally Focused Therapy (EFT), all in the interest of helping people to develop security in their most important loving relationships. I have become an international trainer in EFT, contributing to the education and professional development of therapists throughout Australia and the world, spreading the word about the wonderful impact of secure attachment and positive connection on human wellbeing. So, I think you get it; I am all for connection and for love. The (informed) hopeless romantic.

Working with human relationships has taught me so much about the enormity of the feelings at stake when we give our heart to another and the amazing bravery that is required to repair broken bonds. I feel honoured to be allowed to witness the courageous feats of love that I see before me in my therapy space.

DOI: 10.4324/9781003264163-1

When people risk opening their hearts for the sake of their bond, despite considerable pain and fear, amazing things happen for them and their relationships. I am so inspired by the wonderful humans I get to walk this path with. People are incredibly strong and resilient when their relationship really matters to them. They are capable of humility, of flexibility, of growth and generosity. To see people risk and reach and safely embrace in the dance of connection and resonance that is secure attachment is awe-inspiring. Watching distressed relationships become safe havens for love, acceptance, support, and growth is the fuel for my tank as a therapist and as a human being. When it goes well, when the road has been travelled by these people, it is as though fireworks go off, I go home at night and literally rejoice.

My professional life is all about this. You can then imagine that it is a sad time for me when people who I genuinely care about make the life-changing decision that they just cannot stay together, that they are just "done" and it is over. I share in a piece of the agony when one partner's betrayal of a shared agreement shatters the trust beyond repair. I get tied in knots when people conclude that they just don't make each other happy anymore or that they don't have it in them to keep trying. I ache along with one partner when they are rocked with the devastating news that their special other has left them and won't return. I share in the helplessness when one partner acknowledges that they have caused their partner pain and that they cannot wind back time and take away this hurt. I see the realisation appear in their eyes when they see that what has been changed cannot be changed back. It is heartbreaking when I see good people hurting like this, but sometimes this is, in fact, the sad place we find ourselves in. It is gut-wrenching. It is not what I signed up for as a relationship therapist. It is not what brave humans who gave their heart to another planned on when they set off on that joyous journey of falling in love. Just as a doctor hopes to return a patient to health, despite every play in the book, sometimes the inevitable occurs and they succumb.

A commitment to you...

This book is born from the darkness of the devastation of these precious bonds. It is born of hanging out with the pain of loss, the hurt of injustice, the despair of aloneness, and of wondering how you will ever feel happy ever again. It has grown from the place where you know and yearn for the wonderous feeling of love and connection and yet have experienced the desolation of its wreckage. Dear reader, my sincerest hope is that this book might offer you a hand to hold and provide you with a tiny light in those darkest moments. A tiny light that will hopefully become a strong beam to find your way out and into contact with yourself and the future you want. My hope is that you will feel supported in your pain and that you will find growth and hope from those darkest of places. I will be there with you, as I have with so many of the special humans I have been privileged to work with. I will help you to find some answers to these questions:

"Why does love hurt so much?"
"Will I survive this?"
"How will I ever find love again?"
"Is it me?"
"How will I ever let go?"
"How can I ever trust again?"
"What did I do to deserve this?"
"Am I choosing the wrong people?"
"How do I make sure I don't repeat past patterns?"
"How will I do it differently next time?"

A note on pronouns and relationship culture

You might notice throughout this book that I am sparing with the term "couple," opting to use the term "relationship" or "partnership" most of the time. While I acknowledge that many people are romantically pair-bonded and choose to enter into monogamous agreements of fidelity, others do not. I want to be deliberately and transparently inclusive of all types of relationships, whether they have two members or multiple members, whether there are expectations of exclusivity or agreements of openness. When I talk about partners or interpersonal interactions in a way that indicates only two members, that will fit for couples, but my hope is that it will also fit for the many pairs within a multi-partnered system, each pair being its own microsystem with its own special structure within the larger group. I have no expectation or assumption that the only way to prevent hurt is via monogamy. The concepts we talk about relate to any close relationship, be it romantic, platonic, or a family connection. In fact, relationship structure and definition fades into the background when it comes to matters of the heart. We are talking about something far deeper; we are talking about emotional bonds. And bonds hurt when they are broken. We are talking about how people bond, how to survive the loss or altering of that bond, and how to forge new (and maybe stronger) bonds moving forward.

I will mix my pronouns and examples of relationships, where possible opting for gender-neutral names and using "they" as a pronoun of choice to remove gender bias and to allow the reader to hopefully connect with all examples and feel excluded by none. The examples of relationships I refer to are a collection of the many people's stories I have encountered in my practice and all individual details have been changed to protect privacy. The examples might involve two members, or might centre one partnership within a larger polycule or kinship group where there is no primary partnership, and others might focus on an open relationship where there is a clear primary dyad. The aim here is to include all relationship styles and to focus on the interpersonal connection and deep meaning embedded in each shared bond, no matter the context.

This book is about relationships; all kinds of relationships and the hurt that is caused by their loss. After all, love is love and attachment bonds are bonds of the heart, and it hurts like crazy when they are broken, regardless of the context.

Structure of this book

As all meaningful journeys inevitably do, we will start in Part I by taking stock of where you are right now. Think of this book as a guiding hand at this darkest of moments. You may find yourself moving back and forth in your reading as one section resonates more than another at particular times in your process. Chapter 1 explores why we need loving connection so much and why it hurts so much when it all goes wrong or when it ends. We begin to explore attachment theory and how attachment themes show up in relationship dynamics, either creating attachment security or insecurity between partners. We look at what the research shows us about relationship distress and how partners can become embroiled in confusing patterns of emotional disconnection that threatens their bond and can even sever it. I will help you to reflect on yourself as a person with valid and healthy attachment needs by looking at what might have been missing in your past relationship(s), so we can begin the process of connecting with your deepest attachment needs and longings.

In Chapter 2, we spend time looking at how relationships can get so tangled up that nothing makes sense anymore, that it is just too painful to stay but maybe not completely clear that it is over. We spend time looking at how to understand what went wrong and why. We will look at attachment strategies and the cycles of distress that might have caused and compounded distance and eroded your loving bond. We do this to create a new narrative around the time you shared and the loss of this connection; one where you can celebrate the strengths of this past relationship and learn from the painful parts. We will help you to find a way to use this loss for growth. In this chapter, we will tackle the thorny issue of how to navigate ongoing contact for those people who will continue to be in each other's orbit. Throughout this book, we will explore these ideas together and work through the pain until it is a distant image in your rear-vision mirror.

In Part II, we shift gears from looking at what might have gone wrong in your past relationship to focusing on you and helping you to move into and through the pain of the loss. In Chapter 3, we focus on building awareness about self and connection by learning about your own attachment strategies. We will explore the impact of your most meaningful relationships throughout your life on your expectations and beliefs about closeness, as well as your beliefs about your own worthiness. We look at how past relational injuries can leave scars that might flare in subsequent relationships and how these powerful experiences can shape how you show up in connection, and what you expect from connection. We aim to help you to better know your relational self.

In Chapter 4, we wade bravely into the most disquieting element of loss. We lean into anger and rage. We explore what to do with helplessness and injustice, where negative actions are not taken responsibility for, where no one is held to account, and where you could combust with the unfairness of your situation. We look at how to navigate injustice, helplessness, and frustration, how to find your balance and your voice again, and how to champion for yourself. We focus on the function in your anger, the fear underneath the rage, and how to never feel this way again. This is not a textbook. It is a book about being human with me helping to guide your journey as both a fellow human and as an informed professional.

In Chapter 5, we dive deeply into the grief of loss. We name, own, and make room for the huge pain of this important loss and look at how you can be there for yourself and use others as support in these most desperately harrowing moments. To love another is to leave yourself open to hurt, and when we lose a loving connection, the pain and grief is visceral. We will find a pathway into and through the grief and look at practical strategies for riding the waves of emotion until the storm starts to pass, as it inevitably will.

In Part III, we look forward to what is next for you. Our focus now is on closing the chapter on your lost/changed love relationship and building a happy and healthy future; one where you are armed with self-awareness to know yourself and your patterns, and with knowledge about secure attachment. In Chapter 6, we focus on letting go, on detaching from your lost love, and on growing beyond the pain of this loss. We look at forgiveness of yourself and of the other in order to move forward in a new way. We focus on the important task of shifting and building your support system to maximise your positive connections with those who nourish and lift you up. We will redefine this loss as part of your survival narrative so that you can no longer look over your shoulder with regret or pain but can now keep your gaze firmly turned towards the future.

In Chapter 7, we look at building security within yourself – how to navigate your emotional world in a balanced way and knowing and loving yourself fully. We explore who you are without this relationship and how to be a source of solace and support for yourself. We will together tune into the beauty of your inner emotional world and hold the painful places with compassion in order to mine the wisdom and strength to be found there. We will look at using all this wonderful attunement to guide you to your needs and values so that they can direct your path forward. This chapter is about learning how to treat yourself with kindness and compassion and not losing sight of your needs in your next relationship.

Finally, in Chapter 8, we will focus on how to bring this wonderful emotional balance, self-awareness, and security into your next intimate relationship. We will look at how to lead with your own security, how to detect attachment security in others, and draw them to you. Of course, we will then explore how to create the relationship you want by shaping security in your new emotional bonds. We will consider how to spot and avoid unhelpful relationship dynamics and how to earn security together as you create a loving bond with someone special.

By the end of this book, my hope is that you will have felt supported and comforted in your loss, that you will have grown in knowledge about attachment and healthy relationships, and that you will have increased insight into your own attachment strategies and attachment needs. I hope that you will take this forward into a life of self-acceptance and secure bonding with the special people in your life. That is my wish for you and for all of us; all imperfect humans trying to find our way in life. It is so much easier with a hand to hold in the dark.

PART I

Taking stock – Where am I now and how did I get here?

ONE

Why does it hurt so much?

Let's start by taking stock of what's happening right now. Are you in a troubled relationship and wondering if it is over or just in a terrible phase? Are you reeling from the recent loss of a relationship and wondering where it all went wrong? Are you stinging from a relationship that has ended for all too obvious reasons and asking yourself how to never, ever find yourself in that same spot ever again? Have you recently reconfigured your loving connection with another so that they are now a friend and no longer a lover? Wherever you find yourself right now, I imagine that it hurts tremendously. To lose love is one of the most painful experiences we can go through as humans. It is my hope that this first chapter might help you to make sense of why this is so painful, why it is brave to allow yourself to love another, and why relationships can go so awfully wrong.

I am going to arm you with some powerful information about attachment theory, love, and bonding so that you can start to reconcile where you find yourself now and how you arrived here. I want to start at the beginning by exploring why we human beings are built to form loving connections – also, why we can't help ourselves from entering into the soaring heights and from plummeting into the deepest depths when we allow ourselves to love someone special. Then we are going to look at both what we need from our most precious relationships to thrive in life, and why these relationships can go wrong.

Love and attachment theory

I once heard a colleague say that the most sure-fire way to get into an emotional tangle with someone is for them to matter to you. When we open our heart to another, we make them

DOI: 10.4324/9781003264163-3

important to our well-being. This means that by virtue of their importance to us, they have the power to lift us up or to destroy us (figuratively speaking). Although you may be considering closing your heart to another as an attractive option here, that is not what I am advocating. I am going to normalise the risk and the pain inherent in allowing someone to matter to us. It is risky to love another. No doubt you are feeling all of the downsides of that right now and the benefits might seem so distant as to render them insignificant. Hang in there, this is going somewhere good.

Put simply, it hurts because it matters. When we form a bond with someone, we are letting them matter deeply to us. In attachment terms, they become an "attachment figure." Not just anyone can become an attachment figure for us. We select special people who mean a lot to us, and we bestow on them the gift of our heart. In return, we hold theirs. We do not undertake this lightly and our hope is that the risk is mutual between us and our special other. These special people become a safe place to turn to when we feel wobbly and are a source of encouragement when we need a boost. By showing our vulnerability when we feel small and uncertain, we are placing our attachment figures in a hallowed position of trust. When they hold that vulnerability with love and gentleness, and show us we matter, we are soothed and can go back out into the world with our metaphorical cup refilled. We need emotional connections like this to thrive. This is not because we are strange, needy people but because as humans, our brains are wired for connection. We are a bonding species who do not do well in isolation.[1]

Attachment theory has had a lot to teach us about our human need for close and loving relationships. For much of the 20th century, we believed that children should grow up to be independent and that self-reliance was a goal of mature adulthood. Many people still firmly believe this, but thanks to the revelations of John Bowlby's attachment theory[2] and an army of subsequent researchers examining child and adult attachment, we now know that forming loving bonds with responsive others is vital to our well-being as humans. It is clear that everyone has an innate yearning for trust and security with one or a few irreplaceable others. Bowlby believed that we need others in this way "from the cradle to the grave."[3] We don't grow out of our attachment needs. Far from being dysfunctional, relying on special others allows a person to flourish and to take what life has to offer, safe in the knowledge that they have someone to turn to if things get hairy.

For some people, acknowledging our need for others as we navigate life might feel like a no-brainer, as obvious as our need for oxygen. However, for other people, the idea that we are built to connect with others and to rely on them in times of need might feel foreign or even threatening. This reaction is usually grounded in the experiences you have had with close relationships with important people throughout your whole life. These early attachment relationships teach us important lessons about what it means to be close to another, whether others can be a resource or not and whether we are worthy of love and support in times of need. Our earliest attachment figures' sensitivity and responsiveness to our needs are crucial in developing our sense of security in the world and confidence that others will also be responsive to our needs. This security and trust in others then transfer into feeling more confidence in yourself to navigate challenges. These formative relationships set our expectations for our subsequent relationships, like a blueprint in a way, and impact our belief in our own ability to face life's challenges. They lead to the development of beliefs called "model of other" and "model of self," both of which we are going to talk a lot more about in Chapter 3.

The idea that children need a place of belonging that supports the development of security, identity, and a connection to cultural values are elements of attachment theory that resonate regardless of the culture in which a child is raised.[4] Attachment theory has crystallised our understanding of our need for a "safe haven" and a "secure base" as humans. Our attachment figures perform these two really important functions, and they might look different in different cultures and family structures. Essentially, attachment figures provide *comfort*, and they provide *reassurance*. We all need somewhere safe to turn when we feel uncertain, and we need encouragement to take on challenges. These are two sides of the attachment coin that help us to develop into fully functional humans, ready to live life to the full. If we can turn to a "stronger, wiser other" when threatened, frightened, vulnerable, sick, or uncertain, then they are a haven for comfort and protection – their loving care helps us to soothe and regulate our emotions. Their support and reassurance that we are loved and safe then becomes a strong and stable platform underneath our feet to venture out from. This starts in childhood, in our earliest attachment relationships, and we need it for our whole lives. Think of a small child venturing into the unknown and exciting world of the playground. If they know their caregiver is there and can offer loving and reassuring support if they need them, then they can more bravely and curiously explore this new environment. The moment they become uncertain or afraid or hurt, they can seek contact with their safe other for a soothing cuddle or encouraging word. The knowledge that this resource of comfort and reassurance is there whenever they need it allows them to return to playing and maybe even test the limits of their skills a little further. This is absolutely crucial to our development.

Bowlby was adamant that it is not immature or pathological to turn to another person in this way, believing that this was in fact a biological imperative with adaptive value.[5] Building on Bowlby's ideas, attachment scientists have shown us that the bond that adults form with romantic partners mirrors the bond a child forms with their attachment figures.[6] Our attachment figures as adults serve the very same functions as our primary caregivers did in childhood. In this way, we can conceptualise romantic love as an attachment bond. Partners can offer the same safe haven of support to turn to and a secure base for venturing out into the world, as a parent offers a child. It is so natural to want to turn to your special other (or others) when you need comfort, that we actually never outgrow this need. We gain strength from the knowledge that we have someone watching our back and can then more bravely engage with the world around us. With this knowledge, we can be curious, can take calculated risks, and can put our best foot forward. As adults, we typically get a bit better at soothing ourselves than we did as children with the result that our bonds with our loved ones are more reciprocal (meaning we act as a secure base and safe haven for our attachment figures, just as they are for us). As in childhood, the essence of secure base and safe haven is just the same.

It turns out that there is some truth to the idea of "sharing the load" or "a problem shared is a problem halved" when it comes to sharing emotionally with safe others (especially our attachment figures). Recent research has backed this up by showing that turning to another for co-regulation of emotion is actually the most efficient use of our brain's resources when under threat[7]. If our special person is there when we need them and responds to our vulnerability by showing interest and care, we feel better. These are the most important elements of a gold-star-worthy attachment figure; they are accessible, responsive, and engaged.[8] When we are responded to in this way, we learn to regulate our emotional storms, and we learn that connection is a good idea, and that we are worthy of love and comfort. This does something very powerful to our inner world; it directly impacts how we see ourselves, others, and the world. We internalise this ability to self-soothe from being soothed by responsive attachment figures. We begin to feel competent in managing our emotional highs and lows and we develop a sense of confidence that others are dependable and reliable. Paradoxically, when we know we have people to turn to, we then don't need them as much. This is what we call "secure attachment."

When attachment is working beautifully, there is a lovely balance between seeking closeness and tolerating distance, there is a flexibility in the bond between intimates. When we know that our few very special and irreplaceable others are there to turn to in life's shaky moments, then we can be brave. The security that these connections offer us is invaluable. This does not mean that we are dependent on our partners. This is what Bowlby called "functional dependence" or what we can think of as effective dependency.[9] In relationship, we grow. The more securely we can feel our important other's responsiveness, the more autonomous and confident we can be. When someone can reach out to a safe other for comfort and reassurance and can travel bravely out into the world, we describe them as having "secure attachment strategies." Someone with secure attachment strategies is likely to both be autonomous and able to seek and take in care from another. They can clearly signal their need as required and can confidently go out into the world. They are comfortable with proximity and with distance and can flexibly move between the two. This is what we are wired for and if we have it, we thrive, but if we don't have it, we have a steeper hill to climb.

The downside of being attached to another

What we can take from attachment theory is that it is normal to need others to turn to in times of uncertainty and to use their support as a base to venture out from. I want you to *know* that you are not "needy" or pathological for craving this. As humans, we are wired to form strong connections with others, and we need them to flourish. We are social creatures; turning to others for co-regulation instead of coping alone makes for more efficient use of the brain's resources and leads to emotional security. Knowing that someone has our back makes us braver. Okay, point taken. Attachment bonds are real, and we all need them. No wonder it hurts so much then when you lose a person you love or when someone you love is not a safe haven.

If we let someone mean a lot to us and we place them in the privileged position of being an attachment figure, then the threat of the loss of that connection is destabilising and incredibly painful. When these special connections are broken, through separation, unavailability, or loss, then we will feel this loss intensely. In fact, research shows that the pain of social exclusion activates the same parts of the brain that are active when we are physically injured. Social pain is equivalent to physical pain as far as the brain is concerned, which makes sense of terms like "hurt feelings," and maybe starts to explain why we turn to others for comfort for both types of pain.[10] In the face of the loss or unavailability of an attachment figure, we will fall into predictable patterns of protest and despair. This protest has been well-researched and shows clearly that we all cascade into protesting the separation and then into the despair of isolation. We might show this in slightly different ways, but researchers have tracked a pattern of emotional responses to the separation or loss of contact with an attachment figure, from babies to adults.[11] Some people have learned that spirited protest eventually gets them back in connection with their loved one and others move more quickly into despair and sink into the isolation of individual coping. Through this research, we have come to learn that we all hurt in similar ways because we are all built to connect, and the loss or withholding of connection is painful. We may deal with our emotional pain in slightly different ways but, as humans, we are united in our attachment needs and the pain we feel when it is unavailable or lost to us.

When we don't have our attachment figure as our secure base and safe haven, we are left alone with our emotional storms. We know that regulating our emotion on our own is very taxing and that we rapidly deplete our coping abilities.[12] Without the option of turning to another, we are forced to find other ways to emotionally regulate our inner world and to navigate the world around us. Generally, people with unavailable or inconsistent attachment figures manage the distress of this in one of two ways: either by shutting their feelings down or by energetically attempting to gain contact with another. This means that some people will become adept at self-containment, pushing their feelings aside to manage the intensity and preferring to remain task-focused and practical. Others will become practiced in fighting for emotional contact by escalating their emotional signals to ensure a response from another, prioritising the need for soothing through connection over all else. Bowlby believed that these strategies were "back up" strategies and that they were not as efficient as co-regulation with a safe other, and so were only utilised when this was not an option. We call these "insecure" attachment strategies, and while this term can sound judgemental, it is important to note that we can *all* use insecure strategies when our attachment system is on high alert. We are going to look at attachment strategies in more detail in Chapter 2.

After suffering the loss of a relationship, you are bound to find yourself gripped by attachment-related pain. Whether this important person was your secure and safe place or whether they were unavailable to you during your relationship, I imagine that you know the pain of being alone in the face of overwhelming emotion.

Notice for a minute how you tend to cope with attachment-related pain. Really ask yourself honestly (we often don't even notice this):

* *Do you tend to keep it to yourself, to put it away, and to busy yourself with other things to manage the enormity of touching it?*
* *Or do you feel it intensely and make repeated attempts to turn to others for soothing only to find that elusive?*

This is the first step in beginning to get to know yourself as an attachment being.

Acknowledging that you are completely normal in needing attachment bonds and that your pain makes sense because this relationship mattered to you is the first step in being your own safe place for now. You were brave to have let yourself venture into the turbulent waters of love and connection and you have been hurt by its loss. Now you can become armed with more knowledge so that you can heal and find new love moving forwards. Next, I want to provide you with some information about what makes relationships secure and insecure so that you can more clearly see what might have been missing in your past relationship(s), and what is required to do it differently next time.

Introduction to emotionally focused therapy

As you know, I am a relationship therapist with (sometimes misplaced) optimism about the revitalisation of troubled relationships and a wholehearted belief in the benefit of loving connections (founded by decades of science). When working with the good people I see in my practice, I am an ardent exponent of a model of therapy called Emotionally Focused Therapy (or EFT for short). This model was developed by Professor Sue Johnson and Professor Leslie Greenberg in the late 80s.[13] Sue Johnson has gone on to develop her model more over time by integrating knowledge about adult attachment and bonding.[14] EFT is all about creating secure attachment bonds between people who matter to each other. We will be talking much more about attachment and bonding throughout this book, so be prepared for some remarkable insights into relationship dynamics and your own relational needs. In a nutshell, EFT helps partners to improve their connection by firstly understanding their own emotional world more clearly and then sharing their needs and fears in ways that can be heard and felt by their partner. Sharing emotional vulnerability in a clear way reduces missed signals, misunderstandings, and incorrect assumptions, and it creates a strong and secure bond between partners built through mutual risk and trust. We help partners to feel emotionally connected by enhancing feelings of accessibility, responsiveness, and engagement. This form of therapy is so effective because it goes right to the heart of the matter (where the pain, fear, and longing lives) and works on building attachment security between partners.

EFT is an approach to relationships that works. Over the last 30 years, considerable research has gone into the development of this model of therapy and into investigating its value and efficacy in helping couples move from distress to recovery (the research has mainly looked at dyads so far). In fact, 86–90% of couples taking a course of EFT reported significant improvement, and 70–75% recovered from their distress.[15] The positive effects of EFT on couple satisfaction and connection have been shown in even the most distressed relationships,[16] to both continue to improve after therapy ends and to remain stable over time.[17] We now have evidence that a course of EFT not only changes the security of the bond between partners, it also changes individual partners' attachment strategy.[18] I am comforted that this model is grounded in science showing that it does what it says it does; EFT improves relationship satisfaction by deepening the connection between partners and by restoring security in the relational bond.

I hear you say, "This is all well and good but how does this relate to me seeing that I am in a fairly bad way when it comes to relationships?" While EFT has a clear map to help relationships get out of trouble and into connection, it has also helped us to know exactly where relationships go wrong. This is where the most useful nuggets lie for understanding what went wrong in your relationship and how to make sure you don't repeat that pattern in your next one.

A note on safety and accountability

As we start to talk about what goes wrong in relationships, I naturally tend to take an egalitarian view that partners co-create their distress and share responsibility for the relationship dynamic. In a healthy relationship, all parties negotiate power, such as who makes the final decision in certain domains of life. Even though one may have more skill, knowledge, or influence in a certain area, overall power is shared between partners. Just as power is shared, so too is emotional risk through vulnerability. I see that both partners are equally responsible for the creation of the emotional connection through mutual risk and revealing of themselves through sharing vulnerable glimpses into their inner worlds. In this way, partners are equally responsible for the creation of *emotional* safety through risking to share and by negotiating what each needs to feel emotionally secure in this relationship.

As such, I want to be clear that throughout this book, when I use terms like "scary," "unsafe," "dangerous," and "threatening," I am describing the *quality of the emotional connection in that moment*. I am describing how partners might feel about being vulnerable with each other at a difficult time; when it would feel dangerous or unsafe to reveal your tender underbelly. This is not because you fear that the other will be physically dangerous or hurtful, but that opening up and being fully seen by an important other is inherently risky, in and of itself. Vulnerability *is* emotionally risky, but crucially, partners *share* this risk. I want to honour the risk involved in this brave act and to emphasise its *mutuality*.

In a healthy relationship, partners share responsibility for protecting the relationship from threats and from causing damage to the bond by violating each other's trust. I strongly believe that partners are each *solely* responsible for their own behaviour and their own choices within their relationships, so long as there is shared power. For instance, if one partner violates an agreement of the partnership or violates the other's rights to physical and emotional safety, then the responsibility for that action lies squarely with them. These actions cannot be blamed on the other party or external forces. The relational dynamic might have set the scene for damaging influences to creep closer, but the partner who chose to engage in a damaging behaviour is responsible for their choices. Examples of this are violating an expectation of monogamy or a relational agreement, betraying a confidence, becoming physically intimidating to exert control, putting the other at risk of physical or emotional harm, or using emotional weapons to intentionally hurt.

In some relationships, there is no shared power or mutual vulnerability. Coercive control is a term used to describe a type of relational violence where one partner holds all the power, and another partner does not. This is not an egalitarian sharing of power. It involves behaviours designed to create dependency, debilitation, and dread[19] in the victim through instilling in them a belief that their abuser is all-powerful, capable of violence (without being violent in many cases), and that resistance is futile.[20] A perpetrator in a coercively controlling relationship often maintains power over their victim by insisting on adherence to a "web of rules," by limiting their access to outside (supportive) influences such as family and friends, and by micromanaging and monitoring their daily movements. As Jess Hill says in her award-winning book *See What You Made Me Do*, coercive controllers do not abuse their partners just to hurt or punish them or to seize power in the moment, "they use particular techniques such as isolation, gaslighting and surveillance to strip the victim of their liberty and take away their sense of self,"[21] This is not an evenly balanced, loving bond. This kind of danger is fuelled by fear, which precludes any chance of building security and emotional safety between partners. Where one partner holds all the power and the other is afraid, there is no possibility of building a secure, loving bond. There is no equality in risk, there is an imbalance of power that can only be solved by the perpetrator taking responsibility for their actions and changing, or by the victim escaping the relationship.

In reflecting on your past relationships, we will be looking at their strengths and challenges so that you can learn and grow from these experiences. As part of this process, it is important that you are aware of any troubling relationship dynamics so that you can only take responsibility for *your share* of any difficulties. If you have been a victim of violence or coercive control in your past relationships, I want to offer you support in learning about what you want and need and how to be sure that you never find yourself in a damaging and injurious relationship ever again. If you are realising that you have been hurtful in your past relationship or recognise that you have been exerting power and control over your partners, then it is vital that you can hang in here and do the work of taking accountability and growing so that you can be the partner you want to be. I want to help you to do that.

Why did it unravel?

Unless a relationship ends out of the blue and one partner is completely blindsided, when a relationship flails or comes to its end or is renegotiated, then each partner is usually aware of what was troubling for them. They have usually tried and tried to get the other to understand their viewpoint and felt unheard, unacknowledged, or appeased, and inevitably nothing changed for either partner, leading to increasing frustration and often a sense of defeat or resignation. Sometimes, one partner has no clue that the relationship was in strife, probably because the other was not talking at all about what was troubling for them. What a missed opportunity for growth. Other times, partners compete to have their concerns heard and no one gets heard. Regardless of the dynamic or the circumstances, when relationships break down, it is likely that partners are not communicating clearly about their distress – even when they think they are.

Research into relationship distress tells us that the most common problem that relationships face is emotional disconnection. While it may seem that conflict is what is causing the trouble, often it is the emotional distance, not the conflict, that best predicts whether a relationship will flourish or disintegrate.[22] It is normal for partners to fight, but so long as they can emotionally connect, they can nurture their bond and repair any ruptures. Ruptures are breaks in the attachment connection between two people who matter to each other, when the other seems unavailable or unsafe. When signals of need are not communicated clearly, it is little wonder that emotional disconnection is the result.

Cycles of distress in relationships

How is it that relationships become so emotionally disconnected? In my experience, relationships don't go wrong because people are just not right for each other, they go wrong because partners can't decode each other's messages. Each partner usually feels that they are being crystal clear about their needs and can't understand why the other just doesn't get it. They then come up with theories about why the other isn't hearing their message like; "She just wants to fight" (no one wants to fight – people only choose this as a desperate measure to gain contact or to defend themselves), "He just doesn't care/I don't matter to him" (usually the opposite – it is distressing because you matter so much to him but he is not showing care in ways that make you feel cared for), "She's impossible to please" (it can certainly look this way when needs are not clearly stated), or "They just have to be right" (yes, it can look like this when someone is defending themselves). These theories or assumptions about the other's behaviour and motives become self-perpetuating as each partner becomes more defensive or reactive and less clear about their deeper, more vulnerable needs and fears. They become emotionally disconnected.

EFT research has shown us that partners get stuck in repetitive patterns or relational cycles where the *way* they each signal what they need is experienced by the other as negative (or dare I use the hackneyed term "triggering"). We all do what feels most obvious to us when we are distressed about our most important relationships. Unfortunately, the way one person signals their need can feel threatening or discombobulating to the other. For instance, it might make sense for one partner to get louder when they sense the other's distance, or one might become quieter and pull away when they sense tension with the other. This way of signalling a threat to the connection can unwittingly become a trigger of alarm for the other. For instance, one partner getting verbally louder might be experienced as threatening for the other or one partner's silent retreat might be experienced by the other as abandoning. When under threat, it is normal for partners to reach for their best way of managing their emotional disequilibrium. This is a *coping strategy* that allows them to maintain their emotional balance at that time, even if it doesn't help the connection in the moment. Inevitably, this coping strategy is experienced as alarming for the other and can even confirm their theory of the other not caring/ being scary/wanting to fight/being impossible to please.

I think of this coping strategy as a "protective stance," which is what a person does to cope when they feel off balance emotionally and adrift from their special person. This protective stance will inevitably be triggering for the other. For instance, the more someone turns up the volume to get on the other's radar, the more the other is off-balance and turns away to regulate their stress. The more they turn away to cope, the more the other feels abandoned and turns up the heat to make contact. They get stuck in doing what they feel they must, which is unsettling for the other. Of course, in that moment, they are *not* each other's safe place – they are more and more scary to the other and the signals become more and more scrambled.

So, the two important components of a relational cycle or feedback loop are the way partners signal their distress and the coping strategies they reach for when they are off-balance emotionally. These two factors often dovetail beautifully and ironically in that the very way one partner signals need and how they cope with being off-balance is an exact trigger for the other's coping strategy, which blocks them from being able to respond in caring ways. The problem with this type of cycle is not just that the signals of need get scrambled and missed, it's that *the consequence of experiencing your partner as triggering and emotionally unsafe erodes or even destroys your emotional bond* – your attachment to each other.

Let's look at an example of a cycle between partners to illustrate, Mark and Kate (a cisgender heterosexual monogamous couple). As soon as Mark registers displeasure on Kate's face or in her body language, he is on high alert and fearful of having upset her in some way. Opting to not share this alarm, he busies himself with other things to give her space, reaching for the convenient escape of his phone. He sees giving Kate space as a great idea because it works for him when he is bothered by something. Kate is actually bothered by a work incident, and she sees his lack of response to her discomfort as a sign that he either hasn't noticed or doesn't care. She then feels hurt by this. She would prefer to talk and share her upset with Mark to process it, but his apparent lack of care prevents her from risking saying this to him and confirms her fear that she doesn't matter to him. So, Kate doesn't share her hurt or open up about the original issue that was bothering her, instead sharing her frustration that he is always on his phone, that he never wants to spend time with her, and clearly doesn't care about her. Mark's alarm system is now at 11 out of 10, his fear that he has upset her has been confirmed but he has no information about the nature of her deeper upset. He now feels not only anxious about an evolving conflict but sad that he is so misunderstood in this relationship and that she can't see his good intentions. He doesn't show her his fear or sadness and instead reacts by defending his need to check his phone and by withdrawing into another room. He never lets her know that he is hurt by her reaction and that he wants to make her happy. Kate never tells him that she needed him and that she fears that she isn't important to him. Kate's conclusion that she doesn't matter to Mark is confirmed and Mark's conclusion that Kate does not accept him for who he is, is also confirmed.

This is the sad irony of the negative pattern that partners can become caught in. And this is a very mild version. Notice how neither Mark nor Kate was really sharing the vulnerable feelings of hurt sadness or fear? They each sent jumbled signals to the other by reaching for the coping strategy of angry pursuit or avoidant withdrawal. This coping strategy sent negative signals to the other about their openness and warmth and care. How sad this is.

What was missing for you?

We are going to spend time in Chapter 2 looking in more detail at the types of cycles that partners can be caught in and I will help you identify the cycle that might have been at play in your past relationship(s). To prepare for that, I want to help you to reflect in more detail on your experience in your last relationship (or a pattern of experiences across many of your relationships). I want you to take a moment to zoom out and tune in with yourself. Now that you know more about attachment theory and our innate needs in close relationships, think about what you were desperately needing that might have been missing.

Reflection 1

- *Step back from all the messy details of what went wrong and why, or the ins and outs of the complicated topics you disagreed about and reflect on what you were really crying out for from your partner at a deep heart level that they missed.*
- *While you might have become critical of your partner or shut them out to prevent more conflict or had given up trying to be heard, ask yourself what you were really longing for in those stuck moments.*
- *What were you most starving for that you really could have done with in that relationship?*
- *If you wanted something in particular (like more sex, to agree on parenting, more time together, less spending and more saving, a new house), ask yourself, "If I got that, what would that tell me about the relationship, my partner or myself?*

What need in me would that soothe? What alarm in me would that turn off?"

- *Suspend the part of your brain that wants to use reason and logic here and instead try to connect with the deeper, more emotional part of you that was crying out for something soft and caring from your partner. We are digging for your attachment needs here. Close your eyes and really let yourself feel into this...*

Now see which of these three broad categories best describes your deepest longing in those tense moments with your partner – we are looking for the *essence* of your distress.

Plea for connection:

"I needed to know that I mattered"
"I needed to feel loved and cherished"
"I needed to know that my partner was there for me"
"I longed for closeness and sharing – to be a team"

Plea for harmony:

"I needed less conflict"
"I needed to feel I got things right with my partner"
"I needed to feel free to be me"
"I needed to be enough – to be liked and accepted as I am"

Plea for sanctuary:

"I longed for safety and reassurance (to feel emotionally safe and physically safe)"
"I needed to know my partner had my back"
"I needed to be able to rely on my partner"
"I needed to be able to trust my partner"

Notice for a minute whether your attachment needs are centred generally around a plea for *connection, harmony,* or *sanctuary.* These are three important themes that we will return to throughout this book. Of course, these are all important elements in a relationship, and we need all of them to feel connected as a partnership and to flourish as an individual. However, generally we will lean slightly more towards one of these themes, especially when a relationship has become distressed. This gives us a clue about your attachment needs.

We are going to build upon these themes as we go, but this is the first step in cutting through the details and beginning to get to know yourself as an attachment being. This is the first step; you are on your way.

Chapter 1 takeaways

- We all need loving connection with safe others who we can turn to in times of need and whose support can encourage us to be our best – from the cradle to the grave.
- We are wired for connection; it is vital for our survival; it is not immature or dependent to rely on special others; in fact, it helps us to be more autonomous.
- Attachment figures are not just anyone; they are special. They are responsive, accessible, and engaged. They are there when we call; they are caring, protective, and comforting, and their belief in us builds our ability to challenge ourselves.
- It is risky letting someone matter that much; with great love comes great risk of pain.
- Being responded to by a loving and supportive attachment figure builds our belief in the value of turning to others and our belief in our worthiness of love and support.
- It hurts when attachment figures are unresponsive due to unavailability, disconnection, distance, or loss.
- EFT has shown that relationship distress comes from emotional disconnection and insecurity in the relational bond.
- In distressed relationships, partners become caught in a negative pattern or cycle where their attachment needs and fears become jumbled up and unclear and their way of coping with the distress of the disconnection is triggering for the other.
- This cycle or negative pattern defines the relationship as insecure; partners are not each other's safe haven or secure base at that time. Over time, these cycles erode the connection.
- Tuning into your own emotional reactions and the attachment needs embedded in them is the first step to making sense of where it went wrong in past relationships and in fostering security in those moving forwards.

Notes

1. Berscheid, E. (2003). The human's greatest strength: Other humans. In U. M. Staudinger (Ed.), *A psychology of human strengths:*

Fundamental questions and future directions for a positive psychology (pp. 37–47). Washington, DC: American Psychological Association.

2. Bowlby, J. (1969/1982). *Attachment and loss: Volume 1 attachment*. New York, NY: Basic Books.

3. Bowlby, J. (1979). *The making and breaking of affectional bonds*. London: Tavistock.

4. Choate, P. W., CrazyBull, B., Lindstrom, D., & Lindstrom, G. (2020). Where do we go from here? Ongoing colonialism from attachment theory. *Aotearoa New Zealand Social Work, 32*(1), 32–44.

5. Bowlby, J. (1988). *A secure base*. New York, NY: Basic Books.

6. Shaver, P. R., & Hazan, C. (1988). A biased overview of the study of love. *Journal of Social and Personal Relationships, 5*(4), 473–501.

7. Coan, J. A., & Sbarra, D. A. (2015). Social baseline theory: The social regulation of risk and effort. *Current Opinion in Psychology, 1*, 87–89.

8. Johnson, S. M. (2008). *Hold me tight: Seven conversations for a lifetime of love*. NY: Little, Brown.

9. Shaver P. R., & Mikulincer, M. (2016). *Attachment in adulthood: Structure, dynamics and change* (2nd ed.). New York: The Guilford Press.

10. Eisenberger, N. I., Lieberman, M. D., & Williams, K. D. (2003). Does rejection hurt? An fMRI study of social exclusion. *Science, 302*(5643), 290–292.

11. Tronick, E., Als, H., Adamson, L., Wise, S., & Brazelton, T. B. (1978). The infant's response to entrapment between contradictory messages in face-to-face interaction. *Journal of the American Academy of Child and Adolescent Psychiatry, 17*(1), 1–13.

12. Coan, J. A., & Sbarra, D. A. (2015). Social baseline theory: The social regulation of risk and effort. *Current Opinion in Psychology, 1*, 87–89.

13. Greenberg, L. S., & Johnson, S. M. (1988). *Emotionally focused therapy for couples*. New York, NY: Guildford Press.

14. Johnson, S. M. (2020). *The practice of emotionally focused couples therapy: Creating connection* (3rd ed.). New York: Routledge. (1st ed. 1996).

15. Johnson, S. M., Hunsley, J., Greenberg, L. S., & Schindler, D. (1999). The effects of emotionally focused marital therapy: A meta-analysis. *Journal of Clinical and Counselling Psychology, 6*(1), 67–79.

16. Dagleish, T., Johnson, S. M., Burgess Moser, M., Wiebe, S. A., & Tasca, G. (2015). Predicting key change events in emotionally focused couple therapy. *Journal of Marital and Family Therapy, 41*(3), 260–275.

17. Johnson, S. M., & Talitman, E. (1997). Predictors of success in emotionally focused marital therapy. *Journal of Marital & Family Therapy, 23*(2), 135–152.

18. Wiebe, S. A., Johnson, S. M., Lafontaine, M., Burgess Moser, M., Dalgleish, T. L., & Tasca, G. A. (2016). Two-year follow-up outcomes in emotionally focused couple therapy: An investigation of relationship satisfaction and attachment trajectories. *Journal of Marital and Family Therapy, 43*(2), 227–244.
19. Biderman, A. D. (1957). Communist attempts to elicit false confessions from Air Force prisoners of war. *Bulletin of the New York Academy of Medicine, 33*(9), 616–625.
20. Herman, J. (2015). *Trauma and recovery: The aftermath of violence – From domestic abuse to political terror.* New York, NY: Basic Books.
21. Hill, J. (2019). *See what you made me do: Power, control and domestic abuse.* Carlton: Black Incorporated.
22. Gottman, J. M. (2000). *The seven principles for making marriage work.* New York: Three Rivers Press.

TWO

Where did it all go wrong?

In this chapter, we are going to spend time looking at how to understand what might have gone wrong in your past relationship(s) and why. We will take what you have learned in Chapter 1 about attachment theory, cycles of distress in relationships, and your own attachment needs and use this to look at your past relationships from a new and hopefully more positive angle. We will look in more detail at the general cycles or negative patterns that partners can become caught in and how people's own attachment strategies can feed into this pattern. This will help you to see the cycle that might have been at play for you and your last partner as well as learning about your own way of coping with attachment distress. We will break down not just what you were needing and not getting from your relationship, but also look at how the signals became jumbled up and your connection was eroded.

From there, we are going to investigate what is needed to move relationships from distress to recovery so that you can see what might have been required to repair your last relationship and whether those ingredients were there. We do this to create a new narrative or understanding around the time you shared together and the loss of this connection. This will either help you to navigate and redefine your relationship with your ex-partner in a way that enables you to maintain a healthy relationship with them in the future, or it will show you where you need to keep working to process the turbulent emotions swirling around this loss. Rest assured, we will keep working through this process together throughout the rest of this book until this loss feels easier to bear.

DOI: 10.4324/9781003264163-4

Understanding relationship distress

Firstly, I want to give you the information to understand relationship distress differently so that you can reconcile some possible reasons for why this relationship could not be repaired or had to be redefined. The aim here is learning from what has gone wrong so that you might be able to move forward in a new way; a way that is fortified with knowledge and awareness. Remember, if you walk away from a relationship concluding that it was entirely the other's fault, then the onus is on you to make a better choice of partner next time and just hope it goes differently. There is not a whole lot of control in that. The alternative is to walk away and to reflect on how you *both* (yes, *you* included) contributed to the breakdown of the bond so that you can take charge of your role and can learn and grow. This can be hard to do. It requires a hefty dose of humility, which might not come naturally at this point, especially if the other clearly did you wrong. Remember, we are not saying that either partner is *responsible* for the other's choices or actions, but both partners do contribute to the quality of the connection. Being able to reflect on your part in the disconnection is a much more empowered position to be in. It means that you are not just hoping to make a better choice of partner next time, you will also know more about what *you* need and *how* to get it. That is much more powerful, and I want to help you get there. Taking in and processing what I have just said can take some *time* for many of us.

In Chapter 1, we began to explore the negative cycles or patterns that partners can become caught in that contribute to emotional disconnection and the erosion of their attachment bond. We looked at Mark and Kate, who were stuck in a pattern where Kate would become critical when she sensed Mark's distance and Mark would withdraw when he sensed Kate's disapproval, and neither were really sharing their desire to love and support each other, instead, only showing their defensive or protective positions. I want to take this a bit deeper now by looking in more detail at attachment strategies and at some typical relational cycles that partners can become stuck in. This will help you to reflect on the cycle that might have been at play in your last relationship or your past relationships. Research into relationship distress has reliably shown us that there are some patterns that are particularly associated with damage to a relationship over the long term. John Gottman's research into factors that predict divorce in married heterosexual couples has shown us that when partners respond to each other with defensiveness or stonewalling (not responding) or when they use criticism, especially if it is contemptuous in its tone, then this is potentially threatening for the future of the relationship. His research has also pinpointed that emotional withdrawal and the absence of positive emotion during conflict discussions such as shared humour, affection, or empathy predicted divorce.[1]

We can see from this research that there are certain things that partners do when distressed that can make things worse for the relationship and can threaten its future. Now that we know more about attachment needs and how romantic partners perform a vital role as attachment figures for each other, you can see how high the stakes are. When we hand our heart to someone, this is incredibly risky. You are not just entering into a business-like arrangement with a romantic partner; you are letting them matter to you and that means you are open to hurt. If your partner doesn't respond to your bids for closeness and connection and if they seem unsafe emotionally, you are receiving alarming signals from your important other about the safety and dependability of this vital attachment bond. In turn, you are likely to be sending signals that are intentionally or unintentionally (in my experience, it is usually unintentionally) jangling your partner's attachment system and that make you appear unsafe to connect with. Over time, with repeated misses in this way, a bond is wobbled, then eroded and can even be ruptured and damaged beyond repair. You can see these ingredients at play in a small way in Mark and Kate's relationship. The key to understanding where it all went wrong in your last relationship and to not falling prey to the same fate in your next one is getting to know your role in this past cycle and identifying your own attachment strategies; how you *feel* and what you *do* when your attachment needs aren't being met by your special other. Being able to see your part in the co-creation of a dysfunctional cycle will empower you to choose to do it differently next time.

As humans and attachment beings, we are wired for connection. Somewhat comfortingly, we all protest the lack of connection in similar ways. As a result of this similarity, as relationship therapists, we see similar patterns of dysfunction in the relationships we help to repair. While each relationship is its own microcosm with its own intricacies, the messages of longing, need, and fear underneath are remarkably similar. I suppose we shouldn't be surprised by this because at our core, we all share very similar attachment needs. We all want to feel loved, accepted, supported, cherished, protected, understood, and enough. We all want to know that we are irreplaceable to another and that they are there for us when we need them. We all want to take our joys, our sorrows, our fears, and our triumphs to our specially chosen other. These needs are so natural. They are the ingredients for human well-being and the bedrock of secure attachment between people who matter to each other. Think of them as the psychological equivalent of hunger, thirst, and other human needs. Attachment needs are just as important.

Understandably then, if any of these ingredients are missing from our connection with our attachment figure, we will feel this loss intensely, emotions will run high, and defences are mustered. Due to such absorbing states of overwhelming emotion, we are rarely our "best selves" in these high-stakes moments. With attachment alarm-bells clanging, we tend to surprise even ourselves with the enormity of our feelings, the rigidity of our thoughts and the desperation behind our seemingly irrational behaviour. Don't worry, this is a shame-free space, we have all (me included) felt sheepish about who we become and what we do when we are in this triggered place with our attachment alarms ringing. Despite the chaotic nature of this experience, as humans we all basically do our version of one or two things when our attachments are under threat; we either reflexively dive into battle to fight for our needs or we retreat and duck for cover (and sometimes we try them both).

Introduction to attachment strategies

An attachment strategy is the term used to describe a person's way of navigating their attachment relationships when they are under threat. Stemming from our experiences with and expectations of others, an attachment strategy is our way of *signalling our needs* and our way of *managing our own emotional world*.[2] An attachment strategy describes how a person tends to manage when their attachment system fires up into action. When we perceive that our needs for contact and comfort from our special other are in jeopardy, we become emotionally thrown off-balance. This is so destabilising that we need to turn to our protective, coping strategies to manage this threat. These are the things that we do when turning to another for co-regulation is not an option. The state you find yourself in and what you do when triggered like this is actually your best attempt to regain emotional equilibrium in the absence of being able to use the most efficient channel of regulation, which is turning to a safe other. For that reason, attachment strategies are *adaptive*. We see attachment strategies as coping strategies or protective strategies. Coping strategies perform two important functions:

1. They help us to manage our emotions in the moment.
2. They aim to protect us from more attachment-related hurt.

In this way, our attachment strategies are *adaptive coping strategies* that have been learned in relationships. They are learned in your earliest relationships and become a tool to reach for when your attachment alarms go off in your subsequent relationships. While they protect you from hurt or help you to manage in the moment, they don't always help you to clearly signal what you need from your person, and this is where problems can arise.

It is normal to have a range of attachment strategies, some that might be considered "secure" and some that might be termed "insecure." Different relationships can call for different attachment strategies. It is important to remember that the attachment strategies you use do not define you. They are simply your range of coping strategies that help you to navigate relationships. Some will be more helpful to you than others. You will most probably find (if you're anything like me or the people I work with in my practice) that the attachment strategies you use don't fall neatly into a specific category of "secure" or "insecure," but that you have a unique combination of strategies that you have learned over time. Let's look more at some different attachment strategies and how they can impact our expectations in close relationships and the signals we send about our needs.

Secure attachment strategies

A person who tends to use *"secure" attachment strategies* is likely to have a positive view of relationships and connection. They tend to have a sense that attachment figures will be helpful when needed, that they are worthy of love and support, and that the world is a generally safe place, ready to be explored. They are neither anxious about other's potential unavailability nor about relying on another for emotional support. Research shows us that people with secure attachment strategies are likely to have experienced their earliest caregivers as responsive to their bids for comfort and reassurance, reliably there when they need them. They become comfortable in signalling their emotional needs and accepting assistance from their attachment figures as needed. This instils in them a lovely confidence that others can be relied on as a resource and that they are worthy of this care. The co-regulation offered by a safe other builds a securely attached person's ability to manage their own emotional storms, which has a compounding effect on their belief in their own competence to manage their own emotional storms. We know that secure attachment strategies are related to effective emotional regulation skills and higher psychological well-being.[3] Examples of secure attachment strategies are: being able to let another know when you need help or comfort, being able to offer help or comfort to another without becoming overwhelmed, being able to clearly signal your needs in ways that do not trigger the other, being able to ride out inner emotional storms without becoming overly dysregulated, trusting in one's own ability to manage challenges, being able to call a special other to mind to sustain you in a wobbly moment, and knowing that others are there if you need them.

When people tend to use "insecure" attachment strategies, it means that they may not have experienced their prior or current attachment figures as being accessible, responsive, and engaged. If our attachment figures are absent or frightening to us as children, we can't develop our ability to clearly signal to others our need for assistance or comfort, which then impacts our ability to manage our inner emotional world, and of course, we can then struggle to develop our ability to freely explore and learn about the world. Experiences like this in relationships can teach a person that co-regulation with a safe other is not easily available or rewarding, so they must muster up other ways of managing their emotions and navigating their closest relationships. Most humans respond to the lack of attachment security by either turning the heat on their emotional signals up or down, and some do both. What this means is that we either hyperactivate our emotional signals (turn up the heat) or deactivate our emotional signals (turn down the heat) towards our attachment figures. We did this as tiny babies through crying and clinging, and we still do this as adults (but the signals just get a bit more sophisticated – mostly). These ways of managing when our attachment system is under threat and when safe connection is not an option are called "insecure" attachment strategies.

Anxious attachment strategies

People who tend to use anxious attachment strategies have learned that their attachment figures are likely to be unreliably available and they manage this by energetically pursuing connection with their special person to make sure that they will be available to them. They learned (for good reason) that they need to turn up the heat on their emotional signals in order to get on their attachment figure's radar. Bowlby called this "attachment protest," which is a perfect way of describing the intent behind anxious, pursuit behaviours. People who reach for anxious attachment strategies live with a high amount of *fear* that their special person will not be there for them and will reject them. As a result, they are often very alert to perceived threats to their bond. This burden of worry can prevent them from fully engaging in other things; they can become consumed with worry about the status of their relationship because their survival depends on it. We can't just "get on with life" and put our best foot forward when our most important relationship seems under threat, or our safe other seems to not have our back. Understandably, they will be vocal when they sense distance from their special other and will seek contact in any way they can, often in escalating intensity.

Anxious attachment strategies include signalling the need for safe contact with the other by protesting perceived distance, increasing the intensity of the plea for connection through raising your voice or using more evocative language, clinging, escalating demands, or becoming critical. Anxious attachment strategies can also include scanning for possible threats to the relationship (born of worry about possible abandonment), seeking reassurance that you are loved, and throwing lots of energy at the problem of the disconnection. Because anxious attachment strategies involve turning up the emotional heat, you can be perceived by others as overwhelming, confrontational, irrational, or intimidating. These attachment strategies are driven by fear of the loss of connection. As a result, the special other's lack of response is unbearable. People who use anxious attachment strategies see *connection* as the solution to their emotional uncertainty and aim to desperately seek it to soothe their jangling attachment alarms.

Avoidant attachment strategies

Avoidant attachment strategies help a person to turn down the heat on their emotional signals. People who tend to use avoidant attachment strategies have learned that their attachment figures are unavailable and dismissing of their needs for comfort and reassurance. As a result, they have come to the sad conclusion, often very early in life, that it is not a good idea to take their attachment needs to another – that it doesn't make things better. Instead, they learn to manage the storms of their emotions by pushing them down and not taking them to another for soothing. Without the help of co-regulation with a safe other, they are left to cope alone. This is no easy task, and this is where avoidant attachment strategies help a person to cope when safe co-regulation with another is not an option. This is not an easy feat for any human, and to do this, they have to suppress their need for others (fight their biology), squash their emotional pain, and stay very practical and logical to manage all by themselves. In fact, to help them to achieve this, a person may utilise drugs, alcohol, or other things to avoid their emotions. Bowlby called this "compulsive self-reliance," and sadly, this is an image that is still held up in some societies (particularly Western) as a healthy and mature way of coping. This idea of fierce independence is particularly sold to those with a male gender identification and comes with a side-dish of shame for aspects of their humanity that are vulnerable, gentle, uncertain, needy, or frightened. As a result, people who use avoidant attachment strategies reconcile coping alone as their preferred option and often state with pride that they "don't do emotions" and can handle things on their own. Knowing what I do about attachment, the sense of isolation in this way of coping makes my heart hurt.

Avoidant attachment strategies can include moving away from your own or your special other's emotions (sometimes appearing dismissive or unfeeling), retreating to regulate alone, preferring to stay very logical and problem-focused, going into self-defence, or trying to avoid conflict. Because avoidant attachment strategies mean that you self-regulate, you may come across to others as cold or distant. The function of avoidant attachment strategies is to signal your need for *harmony* by trying to protect the relationship from the damaging impact of conflict. These strategies stem from the conclusion that distance is the best solution to the threat to the bond and aim to "put out the fire."

Fearful-avoidant attachment strategies

Some people use a combination of both anxious and avoidant attachment strategies. We describe these strategies as *"fearful-avoidant" attachment strategies*. These are the result of fear about the reliability of the other's responsiveness and avoidance of closeness to protect against hurt and rejection.[4] This means that a person may anxiously pursue their loved one for contact, but then feel frightened by the risk of hurt in becoming so emotionally close that they then pull back to avoid emotional intimacy. Fearful-avoidant attachment strategies are associated with having had frightening, erratic, or abusive early caregivers who were inconsistent, unpredictable, and unsafe. To have to rely on caregivers like this puts a child in an untenable position where their very natural attachment needs drive them to seek connection with caregivers who do not offer them a secure base or safe haven. This is completely destabilising for a child and severely impacts their trust in others. It is then an act of supreme bravery and endurance for people with this early experience of relationships to even consider opening their heart to another. Despite emotional connection being so painful, people who use fearful-avoidant attachment strategies show amazing endurance when they still seek love and closeness, but can become terrified of allowing another in. They can become extremely fearful of hurt, betrayal, or loss, and can become emotionally dysregulated in the face of such an enormous risk. As a result, fearful-avoidant attachment strategies can involve the sending of confusing signals to attachment figures such as energetically pursuing for connection, rapidly followed by panic with this closeness, and then retreat and shutdown to avoid vulnerability and potential hurt. A sort of rapidly cycling "I want you…I don't want you." This can confuse or even push away well-intentioned partners who long to provide the healing experience of safe, loving connection. Above all else, fearful-avoidant attachment strategies are about a need for *sanctuary* and safety in close relationships.

Common interactional cycles in distressed relationships

Now that we have looked briefly at some of the most commonly noted adult attachment strategies, I want to make the connection between attachment strategies and how partners can become stuck in negative interactional cycles. When two partners are in attachment panic from perceiving the other as unsafe or unavailable, and these two people rally their own coping strategies, we are bound to have some mis-attunements and hurt feelings. It is totally normal, even for partners who generally use secure attachment strategies, to have moments of misunderstanding, to disagree, and to fight. Nevertheless, how these moments are managed, and how they are resolved, is really important to the development of a strong and secure bond. When there is no understanding reached, no willingness to compromise, and no clear solution that is mutually acceptable, then the bond will inevitably suffer. With repetition, partners can feel that their attachment needs are not being met and their bond becomes insecure, culminating in a feeling that their partner is not their safe place.

Attachment researchers have shown that our expectations about another's responsiveness are changed and developed with every meaningful encounter with an attachment figure. Our ideas and expectations about love and closeness and our own worthiness of love and support are constantly being shaped by our relationships. Of course, the people most special to us have the most powerful role to play in this process. Researchers call this a "broaden and build cycle"[5] that means that partners can impact each other's attachment security every time they are safe with each other in a time of need. In this special way, old coping strategies learned in past attachments can become obsolete in new, more secure relationships. However, the sting of this is that partners can create security or *lack* of security each time they are there for each other or not there for each other in moments of emotional need. If there is a lack of emotional safety, then each unsafe encounter is another step towards the bond becoming insecure. Together, partners can build a loving bond and "earn" security with each other, or they can create an insecure bond where partners' attachment needs go unmet.

As we have described, when our attachment call is *not answered*, our attachment strategies are our best attempt to cope with this loss and they impact how we *signal* our needs to our attachment figures. Because there tend to be four broad groupings of attachment strategies as humans, we do fairly predictable things in a distressed moment to cope. These predictable ways of reacting when our attachment needs are not being met lead to the predictable negative cycles or patterns that we see in distressed relationships. Relationship experts have identified three different patterns or cycles that are often seen in distressed relationships, so let's have a look at each.[6] Notice which cycle seems the most familiar to you and which partner's experience most resonates with your own.

Pursue-withdraw cycle – "fire and ice"

The most common cycle we see is angry demand paired with defence or dismissal. In Emotionally Focused Therapy (EFT), we call this a *pursue-withdraw cycle*. In this cycle, we have one partner who uses anxious attachment strategies and one partner who uses avoidant attachment strategies. The more anxious partner reaches for coping strategies aimed at seeking connection but does this in a threatening way that pushes the other away.

This might look like angry "protest" by demandingly seeking time together or criticising the other's lack of response or lack of care. The more avoidant partner reaches for coping strategies aimed at preventing conflict, reducing expression of emotion, and opening up distance between them, which in turn is triggering for the anxious partner. This might look like quietness, brushing concerns off, busying themselves with other things, or defending their position. Think back to Kate and Mark. In their pursue-withdraw cycle, Kate was pursuing for connection in a way that was scary for Mark, and Mark was defending and distancing in an attempt to seek harmony in ways that were scary for Kate.

Cycles like this are like a delicate dance where the more one partner steps forward, the other steps back and the more one steps back, the more the other steps forward. I want to be clear here that we are not blaming either partner or their attachment strategies for "starting" this cycle or for being more at fault. This interaction is co-created, and both partners have an equal impact on the other. One partner's coping behaviour primes the attachment alarms of the other. The natural tendency of the partner using avoidant attachment strategies is to cope individually, but this is seen as a threat to closeness by the partner who uses anxious attachment strategies. The partner using anxious attachment strategies has a natural tendency to energetically seek contact, but this is triggering for the partner who uses avoidant attachment strategies. When one partner stonewalls or shuts down, they shut the other out, triggering the intense pain of abandonment. When one partner feels abandoned, this triggers a cascade of protest, clinging, and pain which is often experienced by the other as difficult to come close to. The more one partner protests the distance, the harder it is for the other to come close, and the more one partner backs away to regulate themselves, the harder it is for the other to remain calm in the face of impending loss. It is easy to see here how the emotional disconnection can happen and the relationship can start to feel emotionally devoid and unsafe. Both partners rely on their best coping strategy to manage the distress between them, but their way of coping is like a foreign language to the other. They just end up tripping the other's alarm system, making it difficult or impossible for them to meet their attachment needs in that moment. What a tangled bind they find themselves in. You may recognise your relationship here (or not).

Alex and Jesse were a same-sex cisgender male couple stuck in a pursue-withdraw cycle where Alex felt enormous pressure and anxiety around working hard and providing financially, often working long hours and studying outside of work time to increase his qualifications. Coming from a family that suffered financial hardship and "didn't do" emotions, he wanted to create a secure home where financial worries were prevented. He saw working hard as the solution. James was drawn to Alex's protective and steady nature but felt alarmed by his emotional absence as he saw Alex devote so much time to his work and study. James felt very lonely and longed for more time together to share mutual joys and worries and to feel close as a partnership. He missed enjoying simple things with Alex and felt hurt by what seemed to be Alex putting work above time with him. James came from a big family where he had to be loud to be heard and his needs were often disregarded, so he learned to fight for them vehemently. As James became more alarmed by Alex's apparent disinterest in spending time together, he would protest by demanding Alex's attention and by complaining that they didn't have fun together anymore. James would accuse Alex of being "cold and uncaring" and sometimes would collapse into desperate sobs as he felt his heart was breaking. Alex found the sting of James's words and the level of his distress unbearable. He felt helpless to solve this problem and coped by retreating more and more into work, where he felt competent. In the face of James's protest, Alex would defend himself and his reasons for working so hard, and would sometimes become judgmental about James's emotional outbursts, suggesting he should see a therapist to manage his anger. This would upset James even more and he would continue to try to get on Alex's radar by demanding Alex choose him over his work and threatening to leave if he didn't. Alex felt in a terrible bind. James was desperate for some contact, any contact, rather than none. The heat of James's escalation and criticism was just as painful to Alex as Alex's lack of response and disengagement was to James. Alex felt that James didn't appreciate him, and James felt unloved. Neither partner felt that the other was their safe haven of comfort or their secure base to launch from. You can see the pattern of this pair's attachment strategies and how they led to their dark place.

Withdraw-withdraw cycle – "peace at any cost"

Another typical cycle we see is a *withdraw-withdraw cycle* where there are two partners who use avoidant attachment strategies. They both are harmony-loving and are both wary of turning to each other for emotional connection, and prefer to cope individually. Both see coping alone as the best way of dealing with their emotional worlds and will withdraw from the other when processing something internally. Problems and disagreements are mutually sidestepped for the sake of keeping the peace. In my experience, partners like this can have very low conflict because both are keen to avoid this, but they will also rarely share their feelings. This means that partners in a cycle like this don't get to "practise" the skill of sharing vulnerably, of expressing clear needs, or of having to repair a rupture to their bond when things go wrong between them. This can lead to a "brittle" attachment bond that does not hold up well if the relationship is challenged in any meaningful way. In other words, all seems okay on the outside, but the reality is, their situation is terribly precarious.

Maria and Lou were in a relationship like this. As a same-sex cisgender female partnership, they had lived amicably together for ten years and naturally seemed to want the same things out of life, rarely disagreeing about big decisions such as where to live or how to spend shared finances. They mutually agreed that if either became upset or frustrated, it was best to give them space to cool down and let things "blow over." Maria had had a very erratic and emotional mother and feared her angry outbursts as a child. She learned to be very small and very quiet to reduce the risk of upsetting her mother or inviting her sudden and sometimes nasty criticisms. Lou came from a family where displays of emotion were discouraged and "getting on with it" was modelled and highly praised. Lou was naturally pragmatic and saw no point in getting upset about things when they could be "problem-solved," and this was a strength of hers. Both Lou and Maria had absorbing hobbies that gave them a sense of satisfaction, with Maria being an avid painter and Lou enjoying hiking. Naturally, there were times when their feelings were hurt. Maria could feel hurt by Lou's sometimes forthright opinions about how things "should" be done and the implied criticism in that. Lou could feel bothered by Maria's inability to keep to a schedule when she was absorbed in her painting, leaving Lou feeling unimportant. Sadly, they coped with these moments like two turtles remaining in their shells. When either felt unsure of their bond with the other, this concern felt too "silly" or too risky to raise, so they spent more time in their hobbies. Over time, they both began to question if they mattered to the other and why they were even together. When faced with a challenge of Maria becoming emotionally close to another painter, Lou could not raise her concern over this potential threat to their bond, feeling foolish for feeling uncertain and busying herself with other things. Maria never knew how worried Lou was or how important she was to Lou and basked in the reassurance of this new friendship, unwittingly compounding Lou's isolation. Here, we can start to see how having insight into our own and our partner's attachment strategies can dramatically change how relationship dynamics play out.

Pursue-pursue cycle – "clash of titans"

Sometimes we have two partners who use anxious attachment strategies and become caught in a *pursue-pursue cycle* that involves lots of heat and escalation. In this cycle, both partners are concerned with the other's availability and seek emotional contact but do this in confrontational and animated ways that can be difficult for the other to respond reassuringly to. Both are battling to be heard, both are alarmed by the other's unavailability, and both respond with energetic pursuit. This pursuit is naturally fuelled by the ringing of attachment alarms, so is likely to be harsh, intense, and may have elements of demand and criticism. When met with this kind of approach, even a person with the same attachment strategy is going to be thrown off balance. Despite both partners agreeing that connection is the answer to their distress, they can battle for their attachment needs to be met, becoming combative or even competitive in their quest to be "right" and to be soothed by the other first. It is so unbearable for either partner to be disconnected from their special person that they can rapidly escalate and not see how their attempts to get their needs met actually block the other from being able to come towards them. In cycles like this, small things become big things very quickly and partners become gridlocked with neither willing to give ground. Regrettably, while they are on the battlefield, their bond is the victim of the war.

Chris and Shae were both emotionally aware, articulate, and fast thinkers. They were a heterosexual cisgender polyamorous partnership who saw their relationship as extremely passionate and that they had a special connection shared by few. They admitted that they had "high highs" and "low lows" and while they were open to developing relationships with other partners in the future, they felt that they needed to be more secure in their connection together first. When they were in a good place, their relationship was loving and harmonious, but when either partner felt that the other had misunderstood them or had intentionally been thoughtless or hurtful, they would rapidly escalate into combat. Chris would accuse Shae of not being committed to their relationship because she was not willing to move in together, and Shae would accuse Chris of wanting another partner because she was not enough for him. Each would rapidly defend their position and escalate into harsh criticism, character-assassination, mustering examples of the other's failings and threatening to end the relationship. This was extremely distressing for them both, and they would blame the other for their lack of self-control and hurtfulness. Their fights could be triggered by any small issue but had the theme of not being sure of the other's love and fearing rejection. Both felt shaky and uncertain of the other's reliability, love, and support. Both lived in fear of the next fight tearing them apart. Their bond suffered from the constant ruptures and repairs, and they wondered if next time they might break it so badly that it could no longer be repaired. Like a piece of metal constantly bent back and forth, it could eventually break. Each trip through this dysfunctional cycle took its toll on them emotionally, and it became harder and harder to repair the damage. This type of pattern can be so distressing for partners because the quest to be heard ends up threatening each person's sense of safety and security.

Complex cycles

Now that we have looked at the three most common cycles we see in distressed relationships, it is really important to note that sometimes one or more partners might use fearful-avoidant attachment strategies and so the relational pattern might look a little less clear or predictable. These cycles are likely to be more erratic and changeable, which can make it harder to see the pattern or the attachment protest and fear embedded in it. This is because fearful-avoidant attachment strategies contain a mixture of anxious pursuit for emotional contact *and* avoidance of emotional contact. If you are reflecting on your past relationship and finding that it doesn't fit with any of these patterns, it might be because one or more partners were using both pursuit and retreat strategies to manage the intensity of their distress. This can be a bit complicated and difficult to get your head around. Don't worry, you're not alone.

Tom and Sue were in a complex cycle like this. They were a cisgender heterosexual monogamous couple who had both

experienced relational trauma in their earliest attachment relationships. Sue had no sense of stability in her home life with an
erratic and unpredictable mother whose mood would escalate
rapidly and could be frightening. She learned to pick her
moments for reaching out and to prioritise other people's needs
to ensure that she had some sense of love and connection. Her
mother was sadly quite neglectful, and she had very little contact
with her father. Sue had been in adult relationships where her
tendency to please others had attracted partners who had intimidated her and betrayed her trust. She longed for closeness but
was so fearful of being hurt and rejected again. She had little confidence that anyone would accept her unless she was pleasing to
them. Tom grew up in a home with a terrifying father and a sub-
missive mother who was powerless to protect him from his
father's threatening presence. He learned to drive his emotions
underground to avoid needing others but had an intense longing
to be seen and heard. As an adult, he worked hard to process his
feelings about his relationship with his father and was determined
to do things differently. He wanted to feel safe, close, and accepted,
but harboured a terrible fear of being rejected. Whenever he
became close to someone special, he would feel scared and drive
them away with superficial criticism and blame. When Sue and
Tom were in a good place, they were loving and accepting, and
could right the wrongs of the past, and help each other to heal their
raw spots. When they were in a bad place, their traumas dovetailed
in such a way that they re-wounded each other. Tom's tendency to
push Sue away tapped into her fear of never being accepted, and
she would escalate into explosions of anger and critical attack, followed by retreat and cold, silent withdrawal. Tom would escalate
in response to her attack, having decided to never to be silent again
in the face of another's anger and would launch a counterattack
that would hurt Sue deeply. Each would feel hurt and rejected by
the other's harsh words and criticisms and confused by their
viciousness and by their distance. It is very hard to earn security
together when the ground is constantly moving underneath you.

The cycle that blocked closeness

Now that you are armed with a bit more information about
attachment strategies, relational cycles, and how relationships
can go wrong, I want to ask you to reflect on the work you did at

the end of Chapter 1. What was it that you were really needing at a deep level that you didn't get from your partner: plea for connection, plea for harmony, or plea for sanctuary? While I'm sure, like me, you want them all, think about the missing need that was most concerning for you and *how you signalled that to your partner* in the tense moments between you (namely, your attachment strategy during your negative cycle or pattern). Here are some examples to help you to see how some people might signal their needs in ways that can scramble the message when they are in a reactive state (we are all imperfect humans after all).

How people might signal a plea for connection

Turning up the emotional heat to get on the other's radar by complaining, criticising the other, accusing, clinging, name-calling, getting louder, yelling, escalating the emotional intensity, demanding, insisting on a response or the exact response required from the other.

How people might signal a plea for harmony

Turning down the emotional heat by avoiding touchy topics, trying to stop the conversation, changing the topic, defending their position, staying very practical or logical, problem-solving, going quiet, shutting down, turning away, stonewalling, finding other things to do, giving up, complying, or agreeing.

How people might signal a plea for sanctuary

Turning up the emotional heat and seeking closeness then pulling away, providing mixed or confusing signals, protesting the distance then shutting down and turning away, complaining and demanding of the other, then rejecting the other's attempts to follow expectations when they fall short in some way.

Reflection 1

- *How did you signal your needs in your last relationship? Were you very clear and non-blaming and non-triggering in how you signalled your needs or were you (like most of us) unclear, reactive, and maybe knowingly or unknowingly triggering for your partner?*
- *How was your partner triggering for you?*

- *How did you feel and how did you respond to your partner when you were triggered? Were you able to send clear signals as you became more triggered?* Of course not! None of us are very clear when we are on high alert, and it feels like our special person is scary or uncaring.

Reflection 2

- *What have you come to learn about the attachment strategies you reach for when you are triggered? Which of the four groups of attachment strategies are most familiar to you (secure, anxious, avoidant, or fearful-avoidant)?*
- *Do you find yourself using different strategies in different contexts/relationships?*
- *Which cycle best describes the pattern of distress in your last relationship? Can you start to see how each of you fuelled reactivity in the other?*
- *Was this unique to this relationship or can you see it was at play in other relationships?*

Really take some time to reflect on this. Flick back a page or two if it is unclear. This is a complex human interaction and not always intuitively grasped. If it were, relationships wouldn't be this hard and you wouldn't be reading this book.

Could it have been repaired?

In order to change patterns like this, it requires *both* partners to see and change their part of the cycle. Owning your own role in fuelling the disconnection in your relationship is really difficult but very powerful. How we signal our needs has a huge impact on the emotional atmosphere between us and those we love. If you can be aware of not just your own *intent* but also of your *impact* on your partner, then this is the first step in owning your part in the disconnection. In my clinical experience, this seems to be the single-most positive indicator of progress. When partners can take responsibility for their part in creating the disconnection, then we are off to a great start in being able to change their pattern and strengthen their bond.

Another hugely important ingredient in the repair process is willingness to step out of defensive or protective positions and letting your partner see a little of the vulnerable emotions that are driving the disconnection such as fear of not mattering, sadness at feeling lonely, or distress about disappointing the other. This "laying down of weapons" and showing glimpses of the tender underbelly of a person's inner world is disarming for the other and invites their empathy. This goes a long way in unravelling a negative pattern and in rebuilding emotional connection. In return, being open to hearing about your partner's vulnerability and altering your assumptions about them and their motives is another crucial piece of the puzzle that allows partners to step out of the negative pattern and to change the emotional atmosphere between them.

I am highlighting here *three key ingredients* that are required to change a pattern of emotional disconnection: owning your role (separating your intent from your impact), being willing to show what is really going on underneath (being vulnerable, which can be confronting and hard), and being open to hearing more about your partner's experience (changing your view of them) without simply being defensive.

As you think about these ingredients, can you see that this might have been possible in your past relationship? Why or why not? Sadly, even if one person is completely willing to engage in the process of healing a bond, if the other is not on board, then it is really difficult and often impossible to fix. I have seen many situations where only one partner was willing to try, and it just wasn't enough to create a change in a cycle that is co-created by both. In other words, it takes two to tango and two to change the steps.

If at this stage, you are thinking about a floundering current relationship and thinking *"Oh my goodness, we are stuck in a really bad pattern and I think we are both capable of owning our part of it, of sharing vulnerably and being open to the other's inner world!"* then put this book down and pick up a copy of Sue Johnson's "Hold Me Tight"[7] and start reading about how to work on and change this cycle! If you think you need the assistance of a great therapist who is trained in EFT, then look at the website for the International Centre for Excellence in Emotionally Focused Therapy (www.iceeft.com) to find one almost anywhere in the world and pick up a copy of Veronica Kallos-Lilly and Jennifer Fitzgerald's workbook "An Emotionally Focused Workbook for Couples: The Two of Us"[8] to complement your therapy process. I will be cheering you on!

If you are not having such an enlightened moment, and are in fact making some sobering conclusions about your last relationship, how it became so terribly stuck, and why it could not be repaired, then you are in the right place. Let's keep learning and growing together. Don't worry, I'm here to guide you.

Navigating an ongoing relationship with your ex-partner

Now that you have some more information about the negative cycles that distressed relationships can become tangled up in, and how partners' attachment strategies can feed into them, I am wondering if this is helping you to feel clearer about what went wrong for you both? You might be realising that your last relationship was actually very healthy, but it ended for reasons other than emotional disconnection. This knowledge is a gift. Please take time to honour the strengths of this relationship and carry them forward with you into your next. If you are seeing why your last relationship unravelled, it is my hope that you are becoming clearer about what you were needing that was missing, and how you signalled (clearly or unclearly) those needs to your partner. At this stage, you may be achieving a sense of clarity about the ways in which you both were contributing to the disconnection and damage to your attachment bond. This can bring a sense of peace and can provide a lovely, shared narrative of "how we lost each other, how we each sent confusing signals that triggered each other, and how it is sad, but we are just two flawed (normal) humans who couldn't quite give each other what we needed." This can offer you a constructive way forward together without blame or hostility, should you need, or choose to be within each other's orbit in the future.

Alternatively, you might want to throw this book away, crying *"we wouldn't have broken up if we could both be that generous and grown up!"* Like others reading this book, you might be seeing exactly why this relationship was never going to work and feeling furious. Hang in there, I've got you – your feelings are there for a good reason and we are going to work on how to process them. It can be really frustrating and disheartening to see the problem now and to have been helpless to fix it then. You might be concluding that despite your best attempts to signal your needs and going without for so long, your partner was just not willing to own their part and to hear your plea. Or you might be concluding that because your partner did something so unforgivable and bond-shattering, that a cycle was the least of your problems – so where do you go from here? I can imagine that it really rankles that here you are reading this book to learn about yourself and your role in any relationship troubles, when it really would have helped if your partner was as willing to be self-reflective. In short, you are right. It is really unfair. It is a total waste of a loving bond and another's heart when only one partner is willing to work on a bond. It is gutting when someone you love and trust doesn't seem to value the relationship as much as you do, hurts you, or lets you down.

In the next section, we are going to focus on you. We are no longer going to look at your last relationship, its cycle, or where it went wrong. The painful reflecting you have done on why it hurts so much to love and to lose love and where it all went wrong will help you to achieve clarity on the past but now it's time to care for YOU. It is time to process the fall-out of this loss, to move into and through the pain, and into a better future for you. One filled with security within yourself and security in your loving bonds.

Chapter 2 takeaways

- An attachment strategy describes how a person tends to manage when their attachment system fires up into action. Our attachment strategies are *adaptive coping strategies* that have been learned in relationships.
- Coping strategies perform two important functions:
  1. They help us to manage our emotions in the moment and,
  2. They aim to protect us from more attachment-related hurt.
- Which group of attachment strategies most resonate for you? Secure, anxious, avoidant, or fearful-avoidant? (We will talk more about this in Chapter 3 so don't worry if you are not sure).
- Pursue-withdraw cycles involve one partner anxiously pursuing for closeness in intimidating ways and one partner avoidantly withdrawing to prevent conflict.
- Withdraw-withdraw cycles involve two partners using avoidant strategies by sidestepping emotional sharing or potentially contentious topics.
- Pursue-pursue cycles involve two partners using anxious attachment strategies, rapidly escalating to ensure the other's love and reassurance but in an intimidating manner that blocks the other from offering reassurance.

- Which relational cycle did you and your last partner become caught in: pursue-withdraw, withdraw-withdraw, pursue-pursue, or a complex cycle?
- There are three key ingredients that are required to change a negative cycle in a relationship: owning your role (separating your intent from your impact), being willing to show what is really going on underneath (being vulnerable), and being open to hearing more about your partner's experience (changing your view of them).
- Making sense of what went wrong in your last relationship helps you to know yourself and your needs and possibly to understand your partner a little more. This can help you to reconcile what was right in this relationship, and what went wrong, in order to learn from it and then let it go. Now we focus on you solely.

Notes

1. Gottman, J. M. (1994). *What predicts divorce? The relationship between marital processes and marital outcomes.* Hillsdale, NJ: Lawrence Erlbaum Associates.
2. Ainsworth, M. D. S., Blehar, M. C., Waters, E., & Wall, S. (1978). *Patterns of attachment: Assessed in the strange situation and at home.* Hillsdale, NJ: Erlbaum.
3. Shaver P. R., & Mikulincer, M. (2016). *Attachment in adulthood: Structure, dynamics and change* (2nd ed.). New York: The Guilford Press.
4. Bartholomew, K., & Horowitz, L. M. (1991). Attachment styles among young adults: A test of a four-category model. *Journal of Personality and Social Psychology, 61,* 226–244.
5. Mikulincer, M., & Shaver, P. R. (2020). Enhancing the "broaden and build" cycle of attachment security in adulthood: From the laboratory to relational contexts and societal systems. *International Journal of Environmental Research and Public Health, 17*(6), 2054.
6. Gottman, J. M., & Levenson, R. W. (2002). A two-factor model for predicting when a couple will divorce: Exploratory analyses using 14-year longitudinal data. *Family Process, 41*(1), 83–96.
7. Johnson, S. M. (2008). *Hold me tight: Seven conversations for a lifetime of love.* NY: Little, Brown.
8. Kallos-Lilly, V., & Fitzgerald, J. (2012). *An emotionally focused workbook for couples: The two of us.* New York: Routledge.

Processing pain – What can I learn and how can I grow?

THREE

Learning about your own attachment strategies

Now it's time for us to shift gears and to focus on you. Part II of this book is all about processing the pain of loss by assessing the damage, arming yourself with more awareness to make sense of the big feelings. In Part I, you have put considerable energy into learning about our attachment needs as humans, how adult romantic relationships are, indeed, attachment bonds, and all the ways that distress in our most special, close relationships causes us pain. Now that you have discovered more about relationship distress and the negative cycles that can erode security between partners, it is my hope that this knowledge has validated some of the pain you are feeling due to the loss of an important relationship. I hope that you are more aware of your own attachment needs and how you might have signalled your needs to your loved-one in ways that might have been unclear, unrecognised, or just went unheard altogether.

We will now take all these valuable insights with us into the next part of the process: moving into and through the pain of the loss of this important relationship in your life, so that you can be relieved of the burden of its weight. In this chapter, we will focus on expanding your awareness and understanding of your own attachment strategies. This will enable you to gain clarity about your own triggers, raw spots, and sensitivities that can flare for you in relationships, and what you need in future relationships to feel secure. We will explore the impact of your earliest attachment relationships on your expectations and beliefs about closeness and your unconscious beliefs about your own worthiness. We look at how past relational injuries can leave scars that can be tender and easily bruised in subsequent relationships. We will discover how these powerful relational experiences shape how you embrace connection and teach you what to expect from connection with another.

DOI: 10.4324/9781003264163-6

Identifying your own attachment strategies

So far, we have mostly been looking at your past adult relationship(s) to increase your awareness of the attachment needs and signals that might have been at play there, and how a negative pattern might have eroded your bond. Now I'd like to take a moment to ask you to reflect on your earliest attachment relationships in childhood. Take a moment to reflect on these following questions. Really feel into them and notice what happens inside for you at an emotional level as you consider each question:

- *Was there someone you could go to for comfort when you were feeling uncertain?*
- *If there was, who was that person?*
- *How did you let them know that you needed them?*
- *Could you rely on them to be there when you needed them?*
- *How did it feel to take your worries and your joys to them?*
- *Did you feel better after reaching out to them?*
- *How did that make you feel about your own worth?*
- *If there wasn't someone you could go to, how did you manage when you felt scared, sad, unwell, or discouraged?*

It's not always obvious to us who these people were or were not. Be sure to hold these thoughts in mind as we learn more about your own attachment history and about your own attachment strategies.

As we discussed in Chapter 2, an attachment strategy is both a collection of expectations about connection with another, as well as behaviours that help us to navigate relationships with our attachment figures. Our attachment *strategy* describes how we manage when our attachment alarm bells go off, telling us that we need our special other or that they are unavailable if we were to need them. Our attachment strategy is how we deal with our emotional world and how we signal our needs to our loved ones. Our attachment figures are special people in our life (some chosen, some not chosen), to whom we turn when we feel vulnerable (scared, unwell, uncertain, sad, hurt, small), and who we hope can be a safe haven of comfort and a secure base offering support and encouragement to help us feel brave and resourced. Our attachment strategies are built over time in relationships with these significant others; they are in fact co-created with our attachment figures. In other words, this is an interactive and plastic process constantly evolving over time.

People who tend to use *secure* attachment strategies are not too thrown off by their own emotions and are able to accept love and support or to give love and support as required. They are confident in challenging themselves, safe in the knowledge that others will be there if they need them. This is because they have experienced their attachment figures to be warm and loving and *reliably* supportive. People who use *anxious* attachment strategies need love and support to help them to regulate their emotions and are unsure of other's reliability in giving it. This depletes their confidence and can mean that they chase closeness in ways that can be intense or even off-putting to others. This is because they have not experienced their attachment figures to be reliably accessible to them or to be reliably supportive. People who use *avoidant* attachment strategies have learned to be self-sufficient and prefer to cope alone rather than turning to another, usually having found closeness to be unrewarding. They tend to push their emotions aside by remaining very rational and practical. They have often experienced their attachment figures to be similarly practical and possibly even dismissive of vulnerable emotions. People who use *fearfully avoidant* attachment strategies want closeness but are wary about seeking it because of fear of being hurt or rejected. They have often experienced their past attachment figures to be frightening and hurtful, so this fear is totally reasonable. This can mean that they can bravely strive for connection and then shy away from it out of fear of hurt, which can leave them feeling in turmoil and their current attachment figures feeling confused about how to be there for them.

Aside from understanding and claiming your attachment needs as a human, identifying and being aware of your own attachment strategies is a crucial step in understanding how you manage your attachment-related emotions and how you tend to signal your needs to your special others. For some people, it is very clear which attachment strategies resonate for them, and for others, it is less clear and may even vary across situations and relationships.

Relationship questionnaire[1]

This is a simple way of seeing which of the four groups of attachment strategies (secure, anxious, avoidant, or fearful-avoidant) you find yourself using the most. Remember, it is normal to identify with elements of all the groups of attachment strategies, but one might feel slightly more familiar than another. It is also possible to have a "global" attachment strategy (across most relationships), as well as a relationship-specific attachment strategy, that is, a different attachment strategy in a particular relationship. It is important to note that this measure was developed for research purposes and, as such, will only serve as a broad guide for informal self-exploration and discussion rather than being a definitive assessment tool.

Read the descriptions below and see which one best fits for you in general and in your closest relationships. Are they the same? Or have some relationships resulted in different attachment strategies?

1. *Secure*: It's easy for me to become emotionally close to others. I am comfortable depending on them and having them depend on me. I don't worry about being alone or having others not accept me.
2. *Fearful-avoidant*: I am uncomfortable getting close to others. I want emotionally close relationships, but I find it difficult to trust others completely, or to depend on them. I worry that I will be hurt if I allow myself to become too close to others.
3. *Anxious*: I want to be completely emotionally intimate with others, but I often find that others are reluctant to get as close as I would like. I am uncomfortable being without close relationships, I sometimes worry that others don't value me as much as I value them.
4. *Avoidant*: I am comfortable without close emotional relationships. It is very important to me to feel independent and self-sufficient, and I prefer not to depend on others or have them depend on me.

Reflection 1

- *Which group of attachment strategies do you most identify with?*
- *Are the attachment strategies you identify most with now as an adult the same or different from those you might have used as a child?*
- *Are your attachment strategies consistent across relationships in your adult life? Or have different relationships pulled you into different attachment strategies? Yes, this can and does happen! Remember, attachment is interactive and the way we express our attachment needs and cope with distress is impacted by the interactional pattern between us and those who matter to us.*

Development of model of other and model of self

The way our earliest caregivers responded to our natural bids for connection shapes what we come to expect from close relationships with others throughout our lives. We learn about the value of turning to others for emotional support and we learn about our own worthiness of love and support through these interactions. Bowlby called these learnings "working models"[2] and he could see that we develop a "model of other" and a "model of self" through our meaningful moments with our attachment figures.

Model of other refers to the expectations we hold about the value of taking our vulnerable emotions to a safe other. This includes expectations about their availability ("Will you be there if I need you?"), their responsiveness ("Will you hear my cry and respond to me?"), and their ability to soothe and reassure ("Will it help to turn to you, will you help me to weather these emotional storms?"). *Model of self* refers to the beliefs we develop about our own self-worth through our interactions with our attachment figures. This includes beliefs about our value ("Do I matter to you?"), our validity ("Do I make sense? Are my feelings reasonable?"), and our lovability ("Will you accept me as I am? Am I worthy of your love?").

These models become a way of viewing both ourselves and our attachment figures. They provide a lens for viewing the world. However, as Bowlby said, they are "working" models, which means that they are constantly under review and are not set-in-stone. With each repetition of a particular outcome, they become more stable ideas about what to expect from closeness with others, and about how we define oneself.

How you developed your adaptive attachment strategies

As a unique and special human, you are a combination of your genetics and your experiences throughout your life. Who you are as an "attachment being" is shaped by every encounter you have with someone special enough to be placed in the privileged position of being your attachment figure. Crucially, attachment relationships in childhood form a template for our subsequent adult relationships. Our experiences of taking our vulnerability to another greatly influences whether we learn that this is rewarding and helpful or something dangerous and best avoided. We form a bond with a special other by showing emotional vulnerability and being rewarded with comfort, support, and mutual vulnerability. Accordingly, attachment strategies are learned in relationships. We learn how to navigate our close relationships as children, and we take what we have learned into our future relationships.

Right from infancy, the people who first cared for you taught you valuable lessons about what it means to be connected to another and about your own worth. Like all humans, as you grew, you will have learned about your value and lovability from your caregivers' responses to you. If your caregivers responded to your signals with love and warmth, you will have learned that you are lovable and worthy of care and support. When a child can turn to a safe other when hurt or scared and feel embraced and cared for, they learn that their pain is valid, that it gets easier to manage in co-regulation with another, that they are worthy of care, and that others are safe to turn to – a resource to be relied on. Likewise, when a child sees thrill on their caregiver's face as they accomplish some new and exciting task, they internalise or "take-in" the belief that they are pretty amazing and can achieve great things. Even when uncertain, the support of the attachment figure can sustain them. When people are responded to in this way, it makes sense that they would view others as helpful and seeking their support as positive. It's understandable that they learn that their emotional experiences are valid and manageable, and if it gets tricky, there are people there to help. No wonder they can develop a sense of self-worth, can challenge themselves to do great things, and that they know exactly how to be there for those who matter to them – *because they have been shown how*. This is the tremendous power of secure attachment. Security, learned and built "in-relationship," is carried for life and initiates an untold ripple effect spreading through every subsequent relationship and interaction that an individual has.

The greatest gift a parent or caregiver can give a child as their attachment figure is their steady presence, care, and encouragement. By being there when a child signals need, by soothing them in their vulnerability and by encouraging them, a caregiver is providing the three key ingredients required to develop a secure attachment bond: accessibility, responsiveness, and engagement. As Sue Johnson describes, this is the A-R-E of secure attachment.[3] She says that this represents the "secret sauce" for healthy attachment bonds between people who matter to each other. It is thought that the wonderful effects of the presence of an accessible, responsive, and engaged attachment figure becomes *internalised.* This means that while we absorb some of our special person's soothing ability into ourselves, we absorb some of their view of us as lovable and worthwhile into ourselves, and can call this to mind to soothe or encourage us when we feel wobbly.[4]

The positive impact of this kind of bond on a person's early development and throughout their life is immeasurable. Attachment researchers have found that there are important benefits to developing secure attachment strategies, both early in life and throughout adult life. People with secure attachment strategies tend to be happier, more optimistic and hopeful, and to be more resilient in the face of adversity. They are likely to enjoy a stable sense of self-acceptance, self-compassion, and belief in themselves to accomplish goals without arrogance or rigidity. Their sense of security makes them able to attend to other's needs in a compassionate and flexible way. They tend to have effective coping skills and to be able to regulate their emotions successfully. When life takes a left turn, people with secure attachment strategies are able to work through their emotions without having to suppress or distort them – they can face a challenge without losing their emotional balance or becoming discouraged for too long.[5] One researcher described this as "hardiness." Hardy people are stress-resistant, committed to what is important to them, confident that they can influence their surroundings and outcomes, and able to face hardship as a challenge to be tackled rather than something to be feared, avoided, or helplessly endured.[6]

At this stage in your reading, if you are appreciating that an early caregiver or someone special in your life right now has offered you or is offering you this beautiful gift, they need a huge hug from you! They are doing you more good than they could possibly know. They need to be applauded for their contribution to your well-being, because so many people are not lucky enough to experience secure attachment with a special person in their lives – while growing up or as an adult. Conversely, reading this might actually be extremely painful if you are recognising that you did *not* have an attachment figure like this. It is so normal to long for this type of love and support and it is so reasonable that it hurts to realise that you didn't or don't have this. The child in you will still ache for this, and it hurts my heart to think of anyone navigating life without the safe harbour of a loving, stronger, wiser other. After all, we are wired to seek this, and we know that it is intensely painful to feel the absence of this.

You might be starting to make connections about how you coped with the lack of this type of loving support as a child and now as an adult. As you become acquainted with your own attachment strategies and can now see the ways you handled emotional moments in your past relationships, and how you signalled your needs in ways that were unclear, this might be a sad place for you. I want to take a moment to honour this place. Your pain at this knowledge is a hugely important step in holding yourself in a compassionate frame. Your hurt matters, your need for safe connection as a child then, and as an adult now, is real and valid. It is important that instead of pointing fingers at less-than-ideal attachment figures, we hold their humanity as kindly as we hold our own. We are not "parent-blaming" here, we are appreciating that all of us carry attachment wounds that can be passed down through generations. We all cope with our wounds and rough edges and sensitivities in ways that help us to manage but might inadvertently hurt others. If you are realising that you have been hurt by or have caused hurt to someone who matters to you, please know that you are not alone. *What we can feel, we can name. What we can name, we can understand. What we understand, we can change.*

Let's return now to looking at how attachment strategies develop by looking at what happens when a caregiver in childhood is less-than-ideal as an attachment figure. Just as a secure attachment bond with a caregiver early in life sets a person up for developing secure relationships in adulthood, the opposite can also be also true. When we do not experience our caregivers in childhood as safe, dependable, and supportive, this teaches us a whole different set of lessons, and we can carry these with us into our subsequent relationships. When turning to a safe other is either not an option, or it is an unreliable or terrifying option, then we have to find other ways of coping. If you remember back to Chapter 2, we looked at how the four general groups of attachment strategies were related to particular ways of managing emotions and relationships. Now I want to start by looking at how avoidant and anxious attachment strategies develop, and then in the next section we will spend more time on how a fearful-avoidant attachment strategies develop.

People who use avoidant attachment strategies usually did not experience their caregivers as welcoming of their vulnerability and may have even been dismissed or shamed for seeking emotional support. So, as a result, they learned that it is safer to cope alone. Managing your emotional world alone is hugely over-whelming for a young child or for an adult. Not being able to turn to another when you are sad, scared, or uncertain leaves you alone with the most painful emotions. Being isolated with this kind of emotional pain is really hard on a person's heart, at any age. So, quite sensibly, people with avoidant attachment strat-egies learn that they simply can't risk allowing their emotions to flow freely or to acknowledge them consciously because they would be overwhelmingly intense, and their aloneness would be amplified. Not having the option of turning to another for co-regulation, they have to manage their emotions by pushing them aside, minimising them, or ignoring them. This is very difficult to do, and over time, becomes more and more challenging, so addi-tional strategies need to be mustered. People can find themselves relying on distraction, numbing, or suppression to manage their emotional world (e.g., over-working, all-consuming interests, not thinking deeply about their feelings at all, disconnecting from emotional topics, addictive behaviours to distract, or using sub-stances such as alcohol or drugs to numb feelings). They will tend to avoid other's emotional expression as well, especially those who matter to them, for fear of becoming dysregulated them-selves. They can become quite rigid in their ways of coping or their choices of strategies to solve problems, not wanting to risk stirring up emotional pain. This can rob them of the flexibility required to adapt to certain life challenges.

These avoidant strategies can allow a person to cope with threats by maintaining an unflappable façade accompanied by rugged individualism – "I'm fine, nothing to see here, I don't need any help." This extreme self-reliance can indeed equip a person with a degree of resilience; however, research shows that these coping strategies can break down under intense or pro-longed stress.[7] The consequence of avoidant attachment strategies is that you can become cut-off, not just from others who could be a resource, but also from the most useful source of information about your wants and needs, your own emotions. In disconnect-ing from your emotional world, you lose your barometer in life that tells you what really matters to you, what you most need. Think of a lone ship, it is fine in navigating calm seas, but if a storm develops, that ship can run into extreme trouble.

Now to look more at the development of anxious attachment strategies. People who use anxious attachment strategies are likely to have experienced their caregivers as inconsistently available whilst growing up, so are gripped by an unmet need to be consistently responded to, acknowledged, supported, and protected. This is such a normal need for all humans, but to have a taste of it and then to be left without it is sometimes worse than never having tasted it at all. This is like a hunger that has been fuelled by the intermittent reward of attentiveness from a caregiver that was never completely satisfied. People who tend to use anxious attachment strategies have never been sure of the other's reliable responsiveness to their needs, steady soothing presence, or their guiding support. They have never discovered their own ability to be with their emotional world and to manage its ups and downs. They haven't been shown how to do this. As a result, as adults, people who use anxious attachment strategies are driven by an unfulfilled wish to make attachment figures pay attention, provide support, and give protection when they need it. Understandably, they have come to doubt other's availability and will be on the lookout for potential threats to the relationship that could leave them abandoned. Sadly, it is common for people who use anxious attachment strategies to blame themselves for the inconsistency of their attachment figure's responsiveness. This adds another layer of pain for them and another layer of urgency behind their quest for the other to respond to them. They need the soothing presence of the other as well as the reassurance that they are adequate and lovable.

When uncertain, scared, or sad, people who tend to use anxious attachment strategies will amplify or intensify those emotions that call for attention and care. They manage these emotions by turning up the heat of their call in the hope of a response. Intensifying such signals has a regulatory function; you intensify the signal for the other to come and soothe you in the hope that if you call loudly enough, the other will come. This is a lonely and frightening place for a human. Feeling like this hampers a person's ability to freely live their life, always watching over one shoulder, ready to anticipate and try to prevent the abandonment they knew was coming.

The saddest part of all when looking at insecure attachment strategies, besides the pain of not having attachment needs met, is that they become self-perpetuating. The strategy for coping with the pain of isolation actually becomes the problem. The protection becomes the prison.[8] Not just because these coping strategies can be triggering to a partner but because they harm the owner as well. For instance, the more an anxious person clings, the more they receive messages that others are unreliable and unworthy of love, and the more an avoidant person squashes their emotions, the more cut off from themselves and others they become. Both strategies perpetuate isolation. People who use avoidant attachment strategies miss all the useful pieces of information embedded in their own emotional experience because they are cut off from them. People who use anxious attachment strategies spend so much time engulfed in their fear about the possible loss of connection that they are not tuned into the other parts of their experience. Both sets of attachment strategies lead to loss of connection with the self and prevent someone from seeing their role in their isolation from self and other.

The impact of relational trauma

I want to spend some time looking at how fearful-avoidant attachment strategies develop. We touched on the fearful-avoidant attachment strategies in Chapter 2 and saw that this involves a mixture of anxious pursuit for connection driven by doubt about the other's responsiveness and avoidant withdrawal from connection for fear of hurt and rejection. Attachment researchers have found that this attachment strategy is associated with having had frightening, erratic, neglectful, or abusive caregivers who were inconsistent, unpredictable, and unsafe. If you have had experiences of caregivers like this throughout your childhood or in your adult life, I want you to be very gentle with yourself now and to acknowledge that this was not right, it was not your fault and that, like all humans, you deserved all the wonderful benefits of having a safe and loving attachment figure in your life.

Generally, a child does not get to choose their attachment figures. They are usually powerless over who they live with, and it is human biology that primes them to seek contact with a trusted other. As a result, a child is dependent on their caregiver for their survival and for their attachment needs. When the person you are compelled to turn to for support and protection is the cause of fear, hurt, neglect, or confusion, this is an unendurable dilemma for a child. It is considered to be a violation of human connection when a child's natural innate tendency to turn to another for comfort and support results in the abuse of their innocent trust and leaves them feeling frightened and alone. Given that attachment is essentially about safety and survival, this is inherently disorganising for a child. This type of early experience leaves an indelible mark on a human being.

Trauma in early attachment relationships interrupts the normal attachment processes and impacts a person's ability throughout life to regulate their inner world and to be able to comfortably use others as a coping resource. Even as adults, traumas experienced in our earliest attachment relationships can "come alive" in any meaningful attachment relationship. My mentor, Kathryn Rheem, says that when a person has "endured more than most" in their early attachment relationships, that the "echoes of trauma" can appear in present relationships when a person risks opening their heart to special other.[9] When people have been exposed to traumatic experiences or abusive environments as children, especially when it has been over a prolonged period of time, it changes the way they see the world. Bessel van der Kolk says that when a person is traumatised, they continue to organise their life as though the trauma were still going on "unchanged and immutable."[10] In this way, new encounters can be contaminated by the past, even if only through watchfulness and fearful expectations. This means that people who have experienced trauma in their closest relationships can find opening their heart to another to be terrifying and can oscillate between wanting and fearing loving connection. They live a terrible tug-of-war between the part of them that longs for safe connection and the part of them that wants to protect from being hurt by someone they trusted, *ever again*. For very good reason, they have learned to be watchful for potential threats and to guard their heart, because the wounds of the past leave a painful scar, long after the fact. When these old wounds are "bumped" in a new relationship, then familiar pain can flare summoning old protective coping strategies (attachment strategies). These usually involve pushing the other away to protect the self from hurt. In this way, pain born in relationship comes alive in relationship. The very act of opening yourself to another leaves you vulnerable to being hurt in the very ways you were hurt in the past. No wonder defences are quick to appear – protection takes precedence. If left unprocessed, hurts from past attachment relationships can lead to emotional reactivity, rigidity in coping, and little flexibility or capacity to take in new, positive messages.

Traumatic experiences in childhood relationships change a person's view of themselves and the value they place on close relationships later in life. When those supposed to love and nurture you are neglectful, frightening, or rejecting, a heart-breaking consequence is that children can come to blame themselves. They can become trapped in a cycle of conflict-riddled attempts to seek proximity for soothing, and then managing the pain of mistreatment or rejection. As a vulnerable child with very little power, it is actually more adaptive (from a basic survival perspective) to blame yourself for poor treatment than it is to blame your caregiver for being a less-than-ideal attachment figure. In this way, shame directed at the self rather than towards the caregiver offers a protection from disconnection and allows the relationship to continue.[11] This has been called the "adaptiveness of shame" and is the saddest by-product of sub-optimal caregiving. Children can grow up feeling unlovable and unworthy of support and then become adults who still carry these awful and inaccurate ideas about themselves. On some level, the child in them might still be protecting the relationship with their caregiver, but on another level, they might be raging (rightly so) that they did not receive the love and support that all children deserve and do not have to earn.

If you are identifying this troubling theme in your life, please know that people with early attachment experiences like this can take charge of their future bonds and can grow beyond their traumatic experiences. People who have endured more than most are strong, capable, and amazingly resilient. The strength that carried them through these difficult times is their asset in taking charge of their future. People can change their attachment strategies and can build security with themselves and with those with whom they choose to share their heart. We are going to do this together as we move through this book. It starts with acknowledging what was missing that you rightly deserved...and then we go and get it.

If you are puzzled because you did not have childhood experiences like this, but you still found yourself using fearful-avoidant attachment strategies in an adult relationship, I want you to know that you can experience trauma in a relationship at any age and can develop fearfully avoidant attachment strategies. While attachment strategies can be relatively stable over a person's lifetime, traumatic events can of course impact them. A person who generally uses secure attachment strategies can become insecure in a relationship that is unsafe emotionally, particularly if they experience a significant or prolonged trauma that alters their beliefs about their attachment figure's safety as a resource.[12] In this way, a person can develop a relationship-specific attachment strategy that might be different from their typical attachment strategies. We are going to help you to work through the fall-out from past adult relationships in Chapters 4 and 5.

Healing relational hurts "in-relationship"

As humans, we can learn to hold our past attachment hurts in loving kindness and can turn to special others for corrective experiences that can soothe and heal "old" attachment wounds. This provides a powerful moment of revision of old attachment wounds and paves the way for building security in your relationships. To allow for this possibility, we are going to learn from what might have been missing in your most important attachment relationships so that you can create security in your future attachments. I want you to take heart from the knowledge that each subsequent relationship throughout a person's life creates its own attachment context. As a result, each partner's childhood attachment strategies can influence how they hold themselves in adult relationships, but their attachment strategies can change depending on their interaction with each particular partner throughout their life. Generally, using insecure attachment strategies (avoidant, anxious, or fearful-avoidant) coming into a relationship might mean that you have a tendency to send unclear signals about your attachment needs, but that doesn't mean that you are condemned to having dysfunctional relationships forevermore. In other words, all is not lost, and things can change for you. Security can be learned and honed.

Encouragingly, research shows us that partners who are accessible, responsive, and engaged with each other can "earn" security together, even if they each used insecure attachment strategies prior to this relationship.[13] People are capable of having different attachment strategies in simultaneous concurrent romantic relationships as well,[14] showing us that each relationship creates its own attachment "bubble." Pain that was created in a past attachment relationship, even if unresolved, can be healed in a new, healthy, and secure relationship. This is what is so exciting about the human capacity for growth and change. Old coping strategies can become obsolete in a new relationship with an accessible, responsive, and engaged attachment figure. Given what we know about attachment, it makes sense that this healing and growth can best happen with someone special to you. By virtue of their importance to you, a special other is bestowed with a miraculous "attachment-power" to deliver a corrective message that has the capacity to right-the-wrongs of the past in a way that no other person can. Hearteningly, we can also learn to give this love and security to ourselves. We are going to look much more at using yourself as a resource for healing and at creating security in your future relationships in Part III. In the vernacular, you *can* teach an old dog new tricks!

Reflection 2

- As you take this in, *what are you noticing about the develop-ment of your own attachment strategies?*
- *What has the cumulative impact of your relationships throughout your life taught you about what it means to be close to another (model of other)?*
- *What have your past relationships taught you about your own lovability and worth (model of self)?*

Really ask yourself these questions, as understanding these things will help ensure the past is *not* the future.

Chapter 3 takeaways

- Being aware of your own attachment strategies is an important step in understanding how you manage your attachment-related emotions and how you tend to signal your needs to your special others.
- Attachment relationships in childhood form a template for your subsequent adult relationships and teach you valuable lessons about what it means to be connected to another and about your own worth (model of other and model of self).
- People who use secure attachment strategies can turn to a safe other when hurt or scared because they view their emotions as valid and see attachment figures as a resource for co-regulation. They learn through these interactions that they are worthy of love and care and that others are safe to turn to.
- People who use avoidant attachment strategies prefer to cope alone because they have experienced caregivers to be dismissing of their vulnerability. As a result of being left alone with their emotional world early in life, they learn to manage their

emotions by turning down their intensity and by avoiding them. They do this by distracting, numbing, suppression, or distancing from them and by remaining emotionally withdrawn from others.

- People who use anxious attachment strategies have learned that attachment figures are unreliably available and so are driven by an unmet need to seek love and care from their attachment figures. They do this by amplifying or intensifying the emotions that call for attention and care, by turning up the heat to ensure that the other hears the call and provides a soothing presence.
- People who use fearful-avoidant attachment strategies have learned that caregivers can be frightening, neglectful, or rejecting. This places them in an awful dilemma of needing an attachment figure who is unsafe. As a result, fearfully avoidant people can be haunted by these early attachment traumas and find themselves both longing for and fearing closeness.
- Although general attachment strategies are relatively stable over time, it is possible for securely attached people to use insecure attachment strategies in a relationship that is emotionally unsafe or traumatic.
- People who use insecure attachment strategies can "earn" security with safe others in adulthood by establishing secure attachment strategies, which can heal attachment wounds from the past.

Notes

1. Bartholomew, K., & Horowitz, L. M. (1991). Attachment styles among young adults: A test of a four-category model. *Journal of Personality and Social Psychology, 61,* 226–244.
2. Bowlby, J. (1969/1982). *Attachment and loss: Volume 1 attachment.* New York, NY: Basic Books.
3. Johnson, S. M. (2019). *Attachment theory in practice: Emotionally focused therapy (EFT) with individuals, couples and families.* New York: The Guilford Press.
4. Mikulincer, M., & Shaver, P. R. (2004). Security-based self-representations in adulthood: Contents and processes. In W. S. Rholes & J. A. Simpson (Eds.), *Adult attachment: Theory, research and clinical implications* (pp. 159–195). New York: The Guilford Press.
5. Shaver, P. R., & Mikulincer, M. (2016). *Attachment in adulthood: Structure, dynamics and change* (2nd ed.). New York: The Guilford Press.

6. Maddi, S. R. (2013). *Hardiness: Turning stressful circumstances into resilient growth*. New York: Springer.

7. Cassidy, J. (1994). Emotion regulation: Influences of attachment relationships. *Monographs of the Society of Research in Child Development, 59*(2–3), 228–283.

8. Johnson, S. M. (2013). *Externship in emotionally focused couples' therapy: Participant's manual*. Ottawa: ICEEFT.

9. Rheem, K. (2021). Personal communication.

10. Bessel van der Kolk (2015). *The body keeps the score: Mind, brain & body in the transformation of trauma*. UK: Penguin.

11. Woldarsky, C., & Greenberg, L. (2014). Interpersonal forgiveness in emotion-focused couples' therapy: Relating process to outcome. *Journal of Marital and Family Therapy, 40*(1), 49–67.

12. Mikulincer, M., Shaver, P. R., & Solomon, Z. (2015). An attachment perspective on traumatic and post-traumatic reactions. In M. P. Safir, H. S. Wallach, & S. Rizzo (Eds.), *Future directions in post-traumatic stress disorder: Prevention, diagnosis, and treatment* (pp. 79–96). New York: Springer Press.

13. Mikulincer, M., & Shaver, P. R. (2020). Enhancing the "broaden and build" cycle of attachment security in adulthood: From the laboratory to relational contexts and societal systems. *International Journal of Environmental Research and Public Health, 17*(6), 2054.

14. Moors, A. C., Ryan, W., & Chopik, W. J. (2019). Multiple loves: The effects of attachment with multiple concurrent romantic partners on relational functioning. *Personality and Individual Differences, 147*, 102–110.

FOUR

Anger and attachment

Now that we have looked more at your own attachment strategies and how they developed as part of your earliest attachment bonds, and we have looked at the impact of early attachments in your adult relationships, we are going to look at how we are emotionally affected when we *lose* an attachment bond. In this chapter, we wade bravely into the most unsettling and distressing part of a breakup. We explore the role of anger in the making and the breaking of attachment bonds, why we feel angry after a loss, and how anger can be both helpful and unhelpful. We will discuss how to navigate the emotional rollercoaster that follows the loss of such an important relationship. We will look at what to do with injustice, when hurts are not acknowledged, and you cannot turn to your partner for healing. Above all, we will look at what you can learn from tuning into your angry feelings, by looking at the function of your anger, and how to find your balance again.

Anger is a motivating emotion that creates movement to protect yourself, to stand up for something you believe in and to fight to be heard. In this way, anger can be hugely valuable. However, we also know that anger can be a destructive force for the self and for relationships. Knowing the difference between motivating, adaptive anger and destructive, maladaptive anger is the key to knowing yourself and to finding the protective and wise message that is always embedded within anger. So, strap yourself in as we explore the impact of attachment strategies on recovery from the loss of a relationship, how anger plays a role in maintaining and severing attachment bonds, and when it is helpful or hindering to your recovery.

DOI: 10.4324/9781003264163-7

Lessons you learned about anger

Anger as an emotion generally gets a bad rap. Its expression or suppression in our environment growing up seems to leave a mark on us as humans. Anger when expressed by a caregiver commands attention and as youngsters we learn important messages early on about the value and purpose of anger. These lessons are often frighteningly stamped into our memories. How a caregiver expresses or suppresses anger models for us how we should manage our own angry feelings. How they respond to our expressions of anger teaches us something about the appropriateness of our feelings, and how to best get our needs met. Unless you're given the message that anger is the best way to be strong and impervious to threats, you are likely to have been taught that expressing anger is a bad thing. Many people (especially in Western cultures) are raised with the message that anger is inappropriate, that it is ugly, uncontrolled, or unseemly. Most people have been frightened or intimidated by another person's anger, and many have experienced the damaging impact of uncontrolled anger. This is especially distressing when the angry person is also an attachment figure to us. These moments teach us how to best manage other people's anger and shape our interaction with our own anger.

Take a moment to reflect on what you learned about anger growing up.

- *How did your attachment figures show their anger? Think back to a moment in childhood when a stronger, wiser other in your life expressed anger. How did they do that and how did it make you feel?* Really immerse yourself in this memory and see if you can feel in your body a little of how the child-you felt. Notice what you did when your attachment figure was angry.
- *Did you try to make things better for them or did you try to be invisible so that it wouldn't be directed towards you? Did you push back against their anger or try to duck for cover?*
- *If anger wasn't ever expressed in your house, how did you know if your attachment figure might have been angry? What clues did you look for?*
- *What did you do with your own angry feelings as a child? Did you express them and if you did, how did you do that?*
- *How were your angry feelings received?*

- *What important lessons about anger did you learn from your attachment figures growing up?*

Note at this point that some strong feelings might emerge. That's okay, give yourself some time and remember to treat yourself gently.

Emotional reactions to relationship loss

People's reactions to the loss of an important relationship can vary widely depending on the circumstances surrounding the loss, their experience with other losses in life, and their attachment strategies. Factors such as the suddenness of the break-up, whether you were the one who made the move to end the relationship, whether there was a breach of trust caused by you or by your partner, whether there were other important stressors in your life at the time, how deeply attached you were to the other, and many more, all play a role in determining the emotional impact of this loss. The emotional reaction to the loss of a relationship varies between people and can fluctuate over time between love, sadness, anger, relief, guilt, and shame, all in a perfectly imperfect way. Each person's reaction is particular to them and might change on a daily basis, especially when the loss is fresh.[1]

As we have discussed in Chapters 1–3, John Bowlby highlighted the importance of early attachment relationships on human well-being and acknowledged the anxiety and distress caused by the loss of an attachment figure. He saw separation anxiety and distress as a natural and inevitable response whenever an attachment figure is inexplicably missing. As his thoughts about the importance of human emotional ties developed into his attachment theory, Bowlby was very interested in the emotional impact of separation from an attachment figure. As a result of his research, he was instrumental in mapping the phases of a separation response in both children and adults.[2]

The first is *numbing* which he described as a short-lived phase of emotional disconnection from the reality of the loss. He noticed that this numbness was often interrupted by outbursts of anger or distress and then numbness would return. It is almost as if in the early stages of confronting a loss of this magnitude, the numbness allows a person to limit how much of the truth of the loss they encounter at a time. This can be interpreted as self-protective.

The second is *yearning and searching* (also called protest), where he noted that people took in the reality of the loss. This caused extreme distress, but they also experienced restlessness and preoccupation with thoughts of the other. In this phase, he found that people were sometimes "seized by an urge" to search for their special other even if they knew this was illogical. He connected the understandable crying and calling out for the lost love as an attempt to call for the missing person in the same way a baby cries out for their caregiver. In this way, he described searching and crying as attempts to re-establish contact with the lost attachment figure. He saw this as a "protest" against the loss resembling a plea to recover and restore the lost connection.

The third phase is *disorganisation and despair*, where the reality of the loss and futility of searching is realised, resulting in intense sadness and withdrawal. This is a time of depletion and hopelessness where a person is likely to experience not only sadness, but a terrible sense of isolation and desolation. This phase is associated with sleep and appetite disturbance, social withdrawal, and extreme depression and loneliness. The depth of the despair is impacted by the depth of the connection as well as the person's attachment strategies.

The fourth phase as identified by Bowlby is *reorganisation*, where the individual is able to process the loss and detach from the lost person. This frees them from the searching for the other as the solution to their pain and allows them to reconnect with themselves and to begin to establish other attachment bonds.[3]

In order to successfully adjust to the loss of an attachment figure, Bowlby argued that people need to reorganise their inner world in such a way that they no longer seek out the lost love as a safe haven of comfort or secure base for encouragement.[4] This means that the continued desire to keep seeking out your ex-partner for your attachment needs is no longer adaptive when they are no longer your special other. This can be extremely painful – we are talking about redefining your ex-partner as no longer one of your most "special" people. This might be because they are no longer in your life, or because they are in your life, but you have reconfigured your relationship in such a way that they are no longer an attachment figure for you. We can draw from this that an important part of working through this loss involves accepting that you are in a grieving process. Crucial to this process is redefining the lost love in your mind, removing them from the "inner circle" of your most trusted and special people and hence no longer turning to them for your attachment needs. It is so painful *because* you are "undoing" the attachment bond.

These important tasks take time, and we can become stuck at many points during this process. Bowlby believed that people become "stuck" in the grieving process when they cannot seem to move beyond the yearning (protest) phase or the despair phase. He felt that this was either because they were overwhelmed by the intensity of the emotions (i.e., feeling too much) or they were not engaging in the emotional processing needed (i.e., not feeling enough). For those who were feeling "too much," they were so preoccupied with the lost partner and their feelings of protest or despair that they were unable to function normally. For those who were "not feeling enough," they were bypassing the important stages of processing and moving straight to the reor-ganisation phase of moving on.[5]

Even if you are the one who ended the relationship, even if you know it wasn't right for you, working through the loss of this magnitude is no mean feat. Even if no one was at fault and you are still in each other's lives in a newly defined way, this is still really hard. I mean, if you could easily do that type of mental juggle that redefines your partner as an "ex" partner, I imagine you wouldn't be reading this book. If this was easily done, break-ups would not be as universally *painful* as they are (and they are painful!). It is well documented that the loss of a romantic rela-tionship is associated with emotional distress that places people at high risk of poor mental health outcomes.[6] Following Bowl-by's phases, in this chapter, we will start by exploring the role of anger as part of the yearning and searching phase, and then we will move to disorganisation and despair in Chapter 5. In Chapter 6, we will look at reorganising and detaching.

The impact of attachment strategies on adjustment to the loss of a relationship

How do your attachment strategies influence the way you emo-tionally respond to relationship loss and what your recovery looks like? I'm guessing that you now know enough about the impact of attachment strategies on how we show up in our closest relationships to be fairly unsurprised to hear that your attachment strategies play a very important role in how you respond to and heal from the loss of an attachment figure.

Research into emotional adjustment after the loss of a romantic relationship shows us that people who use secure attachment strategies tend to face loss with a higher level of resilience and acceptance and that they have a faster emotional recovery than people who use insecure attachment strategies. They are more likely to be unconcerned about seeing their ex-partner again, to feel less blame towards their ex-partner, and to feel ready to date more quickly than people who use insecure attachment strategies.[7] People with secure attachment strategies are also more likely to rely on other relationships, such as their family or friends, as safe havens to help them in their emotional adjustment to the loss.[8] Of course, those people who use insecure attachment strategies might have other factors that affect their ability to cope, socio-culturally, economically, domestically, and so on.

People who use insecure attachment strategies seem to be more likely to struggle emotionally after a relationship loss. Both anxious and avoidant attachment strategies are related to higher levels of distress during the recovery from a loss in people using them than people with secure attachment strategies, and they are more likely to use drugs or alcohol to cope. Despite these similarities, there are some clear differences between those with anxious attachment strategies and those with avoidant attachment strategies. People who use *anxious* attachment strategies have been found to think more about their lost partner, often becoming preoccupied with thoughts about the loss and reporting high levels of emotional distress. Their high levels of distress are attributed to the amplification of their signals of need and their tendency to keep turning to their ex-partner for safe haven and secure base needs even though the relationship is over.[9] They are more likely to make strenuous attempts to make contact with their ex-partner and to try to repair the bond. They can also become emotionally elevated, sometimes blaming themselves for the loss, and at other times expressing anger or even vengeful behaviours towards their ex-partner. The impact of this loss for a person who uses anxious attachment strategies is monumental, absorbing vast quantities of vital emotional energy and diminishing their ability to connect with other important parts of their life. Given what we know about people with anxious attachment strategies, it makes sense that separation from a loved one is excruciating and that there is a considerable urge to keep seeking the other out for comfort and reassurance. It is just sad that the other can no longer be the source of love, support, and comfort and so those unbearable emotions go un-soothed. Significant mental health challenges may be faced as a result.

In contrast, people with *avoidant* attachment strategies tend to display lower levels of distress about the separation than those who use anxious attachment strategies. They are also less likely to engage in contact with their ex-partner or to attempt to reconcile and are more likely to use self-reliant coping strategies. This stands to reason given their tendency to distance themselves from their more vulnerable emotions and to remain practical; it could easily be concluded that they are adjusting well to the loss of the relationship. It appears that the more a person thinks about the loss of a relationship and attempts to turn to their ex-partner for attachment-related support after such a loss, the more distress they are likely to feel, and feel for a longer time after a relationship dissolution.[10] Because people who use avoidant attachment strategies are less likely to do these things, they might progress very quickly to the reorganisation phase. However, this does not mean that they are coping as well on the inside as they might outwardly appear. Some researchers have found that those who use avoidant attachment strategies had negative responses to a relationship loss compared to individuals who use secure strategies that included self-blame, reduced motivation to look for a new partner, and reduced interest in sex. Other researchers have shown that those with avoidant attachment strategies displayed poorer post-divorce emotional well-being and adjustment than did those with secure attachment strategies. So, it appears that some significant losses can penetrate through the defences of people who use avoidant attachment strategies.[11] This is understandable, given what we know about individual coping and its relative expiry date. If a stressor is meaningful enough and prolonged enough, eventually the effort of coping alone will deplete a person's natural resources and they will struggle to stem the tide of vulnerable emotion.

The role of anger in attachment

Together, we have established that our attachment strategies influence how we experience the pain of a severed bond and impact our approach to managing the loss of an attachment figure. We can see from the research that people with anxious attachment strategies are likely to experience extreme levels of anxiety and distress during a separation. They are also likely to outwardly express more distress about the loss and to keep turning to their ex-partner in a bid for reassurance or soothing from them. It is really hard to carry the pain of the loss alone when you have learned over your whole life to take your pain to the person who can help you with it. It is especially hard to no longer seek this when you have experienced your attachment figures to be inconsistently available; their previously intermittent care only fuels the effort to engage the other and keeps a tiny spark of hope alive when it might no longer be warranted. No wonder those with anxious attachment strategies keep trying to turn to their ex-partner after a relationship ends. No wonder they keep energetically trying to repair the bond, to resolve the hurt, or to seek something they need from the other.

That said, partners with anxious attachment strategies are not alone in becoming very distressed following an unwanted or unexpected breakup. I have seen many people with avoidant attachment strategies who become mobilised with the threat of the loss of their important relationship and who move into what we call "reactive pursuit."[12] In this state, they show many of the same protest behaviours that partners with anxious strategies display as well as showing high levels of distress. While some partners with avoidant attachment strategies might retreat into self-reliant coping and steer clear of contact with their ex-partner, some might find themselves in the unfamiliar territory of urgently pursuing their lost love. This is because their protective strategy of self-reliance can break down in the face of such a significant stressor like losing your partner. Coping alone is a fragile and time-limited strategy, which can crumble if the stress exceeds your ability to hang in there alone. Becoming angry in your attempt to be heard in your protest about the ending of this important relationship, or to have your needs met, is a natural way of trying to create change. The way you do that is vital. Urgent pursuit isn't always effective because the delivery of the message might be unclear or aversive for the other, preventing your message from landing. This can then leave you feeling even worse. However, the spirit of your anger and protest will be coming from a really important place that we need to tune into.

If you identify with this, please don't be harsh with yourself. Try to hold on to Bowlby's thoughts about protest and yearning and searching. The amplification of your painful emotions is your well-intentioned attempt to reach your lost love and to seek what you need from them to heal. Sometimes, what you need may be very clear, and at other times, this might be elusive. For instance, you might know that what you need is to get back together, or you might need something less tangible such as recognition for your efforts or acknowledgement of a hurt inflicted on you. Sometimes, it might be possible for your ex-partner to provide this so long as your signals are clear, and at other times, it is not possible that you will ever receive what you are needing from them. Regardless of the good intention behind your anger, it is vital to note that there is no excuse for threatening, intimidating, or aggressive behaviours towards another person. We are going to work through this together, so that you can find the meaning behind your frustrated feelings, and so that you can be honest with yourself about when they are healthy or unhealthy. No one wants to become someone they don't recognise when reactive and angry, even if it is coming from a well-intentioned or triggered place.

Bowlby said that the anger a person feels following a loss can be the "anger of hope." When directed at the partner, he saw this as a reproach for the other having been absent when they were needed, and that it was intended to remind them not to err again. When a loss is short-term and can be repaired, then anger can be a healthy way of overcoming obstacles to the special other, signalling hurt feelings, and initiating the process of reconnection. In this way, anger can play an important role in promoting the bond and restoring it after a rupture. This is an example of *helpful* anger. For example, the angry reproach a parent feels when their child runs off in the supermarket commands the child's attention and acts as a deterrent from straying too far from the parent again. However, if the loss is not retrievable, then the anger of hope is without purpose and can even become destructive to oneself and the other. He believed that this is when it becomes the "anger of despair." Bowlby felt that our attachment system compelled us to keep searching for a lost love, even when there is no hope of recovery, for a while at least. He normalised the anger of hope and the anger of despair as part of a bereavement process, which does eventually move to a resolution. How long this process takes varies between people. He was clear that anger became dysfunctional when it weakened the attachment bond and began to alienate or demoralise the partner rather than promoting the safe haven and secure base functions of safe connection. He gave examples of dysfunctional anger such as becoming vengeful, exerting coercion, showing hostility or hate – as he felt that these eroded the love.[13] These are examples of unhelpful or destructive anger.

As you think about the function of anger, I wonder what you are noticing about your own angry feelings in response to this loss. I want to ask you to reflect on your relationship with anger (without harsh self-judgement) and then we will listen to what it is trying to tell you.

- *How do you feel about anger in close relationships?*
- *How have your past partners expressed anger and how did this affect you?*
- *Do you freely express angry feelings with a partner? How do you do this?*
- *How have they responded to your anger in the past?*
- *How do you feel about how you have expressed anger in the past?*
- *How are you expressing anger now that you have separated from your partner/redefined your relationship?*

Healthy versus unhealthy anger

We need to firstly honour your anger and find the function in it so that we can ascertain what you are longing for and how to best achieve this, either from your ex-partner, from others in your life, or from yourself. The rest of this book is concerned with this process so let's take it one step at a time. The aim is not to criticise or judge, but to promote your self-understanding.

Anger is a protective and mobilising emotion. The action tendency of anger is to move towards, to change, to challenge, to set limits, to stand and fight for what is right. In my experience, people get angry in two ways: a sudden flare in reaction to other deeper feelings or a slow-burn to take a firm and assertive stand. The first way involves using anger to protect themselves from feeling something they don't want to feel, such as ashamed, small, silly, weak, vulnerable, faulty, scared, or helpless. In this way, hot anger acts like a wall of fire to prevent anyone from getting too close, to chase away bad feelings, and to feel a little more powerful or capable when in fact a person feels just the opposite. We call this "reactive" emotion. It is fast, it is intense, and it is on the surface. It often *masks something deeper* and more vulnerable, and it often causes damage to relationships.

The other way people express anger is slower and more measured, like a slow and powerful burn. This type of anger is calm and assertive, and it is used to move a person in the service of what is right for them. This type of emotion is what we call "primary." Primary emotion is the most important and meaningful type of emotion because it comes right from the heart of our emotional world and is embedded in rich meaning about what is most important to us. When tuned into, our *primary emotions tell us exactly what we most need*. When shared vulnerably and clearly, primary emotion bonds people together. The catch is that in order to get to our primary emotions, we have to be with ourselves, we have to tune in and pay attention to the delicate emotional music of our inner world. This is no easy feat if you have never been shown how to be with your own emotions, or if what you find there is frightening or uncomfortable. When primary emotion feels scary or overwhelming, of course it feels so much better to move away from these feelings.

In general terms, there are only six to eight core, primary emotions (it depends on the exact definition) and they are joy (including happiness and love), sadness, anger, fear, shame (sometimes expanded to guilt and disgust), and surprise (including curiosity).[14] These emotions are universal, and they are vital for our survival because they urge us to explore, to gather and defend resources, to reproduce, to care for others, to protect ourselves from danger, to maintain social contact, to bond with others, and to grieve. They are a highly evolved signalling system within ourselves and between us and our social group.[15] Aside from joy and surprise, these are some of the most difficult feelings to be with, and it is no wonder that as humans, we find it hard to stay with them for too long, if at all. This is why we have protective coping strategies that swoop in and take us away from these emotions. Often our reactive emotions help us to move away or to manage our more primary experiences. Reactive emotions also can push other people away because they are interested in shielding yourself, not in opening up to another, nor in seeing or being seen. This is sometimes helpful in the moment, but the consequence is that primary emotions can be ignored. When we ignore or disown our primary emotions, we cut ourselves off from a rich source of information about our deepest needs and fears. Until a person acknowledges these, you could say any reactive emotion has the potential to be detrimental. Sometimes, our primary emotions lay dormant and untapped, their wisdom about our needs going unread. At other times, ignored primary emotion intensifies and becomes harder to suppress and manage. A bit like putting a cap on a volcano.

Therefore, as an analogy, I like to think of primary and reactive emotions in terms of a volcano. If you visualise that the primary emotions live at the core of the volcano, right at the centre of our world, they are full of meaning that is waiting for us to tap into. If a volcano has a plug blocking the lava from erupting through the main vent, then given the building pressure, the lava has to squirt out in other directions through any point of weakness in the rock surface (I think they're called vents – bear with me, I'm not a geologist after all). These smaller eruptions go off in unpredictable directions and might look unconnected to the main volcano. Alternatively, so much pressure builds up that eventually the lava bursts forth from the main vent with enough force to blow out the plug. If we think of primary emotion as the lava sitting in the core of the volcano, then the reactive emotion is the lava spraying from the main vent or from the side vents.

To illustrate what I mean, imagine that someone is really afraid of being hurt by their partner. They have primary fear that is very understandable for us all; however, for them, it feels even more frightening and risky because they have been betrayed and abandoned before in a close relationship. As a result, they don't like to touch their fear, so they squash it down and avoid it and certainly do not consider sharing it with their partner. The pressure of this unshared and unexplored fear builds like lava in the bottom of the volcano. They cap it off, telling themselves that the fear is silly, that their partner will think less of them if they share it, and the pressure builds. Over time, the fear squirts out of the vents in small ways that look like snappiness and irritability, irrational questioning over their partner's devotion, and using alcohol (or medication or drugs) to relieve pressure. This puts their partner on edge and starts to wobble the partnership connection. Despite this, it is easier to get angry about small disappointments than to share the bigger fear. As the pressure builds in the volcano, eventually the cap blows, and the reactive emotion bursts forth as a gush of rage and jealousy about their partner's attractive workmate who they are sure is being flirtatious. This overwhelming emotional flood is obviously extremely upsetting for all parties, and the real nub of the primary emotion only finally comes out in the sea of hurt feelings and reproach. In this way, the pressure in the "volcano" was only released in a destructive way, and an opportunity for bonding over shared vulnerability was only partially offered. The fall-out from reactive emotion spraying around was damaging to the attachment bond.

Finding the wisdom in anger

Now that we are thinking a bit more about reactive and primary anger, I want to stay with any angry feelings you may have, so that we can explore them and find the meaning in them. People don't usually get angry without a reason, sometimes we need to lean in and really listen to find it, but it is always there. Anger is such a useful signal for us to pay attention to our core emotions and needs. Let's explore how to do this together.

Reactive emotion is damaging to a connection because it is confusing, unclear, and sometimes hurtful. The things we do when we are in reactive anger are rarely positive for the connection or for the other person. Reactive anger misses the real meaning about our deepest wants and needs and is only concerned with managing discomfort in the moment. We are responsible entirely for our actions when reactive, and in this state, we are more likely to be frightening to those we care about. Being angry isn't an excuse for being aggressive, threatening, intimidating, or hurtful. It is important that we can own this, even though it is really difficult, and take complete responsibility for our actions when angry. This is the only way to learn from them and to ensure that you don't bring this dynamic into your next relationship. As you reflect on any angry feelings as a result of this relationship loss, can you ask yourself about the function of your anger? The best way to tune into and learn from your angry feelings is to listen to the *spirit* of them and to hear the message of *need* that will be there. I am asking you to dig right to the bottom of the volcano, to find what the need is, to find the fear and the vulnerability that is behind the reactive anger you are feeling now. Often reactive anger masks hurt, sadness, fear, or shame. Once you can get to that most meaningful place, then we can work with that to honour what we find there. To go on this journey, imagine you are taking the elevator down into your emotional experience, level by level until we get to the basement where the richest source of meaning can be found.

Top floor – Noticing and attending

Firstly, we need to slow down and connect with these reactive feelings, knowing that there is something important for us to attend to in them. To do this, ask yourself:

- *Is your anger reactive, hot, fast, and other-directed?*
- *What seems to <u>trigger</u> these feelings?*
- *What sensations do you notice in your <u>body</u> when these feelings flare?*
- *What do you <u>tell yourself</u> as you are feeling these angry feelings?*
- *What is the <u>meaning</u> you are making about the situation, your ex-partner, or yourself?*

Then notice how you tend to manage these feelings, and what action they predictably lead to.

- *What do you typically <u>do</u> to manage the intensity of these feelings? What actions are you driven to take when you feel this way?*

As you assemble the pieces of this experience, by exploring in this way, we know that big feelings become more ordered and a little easier to have. Sue Johnson describes this process as "emotion assembly," and it is a very useful strategy for tuning into your emotional experience rather than turning away from it.[16]

Ground floor – Finding the function

Now that you have assembled the fragments of your reactive emotional experience, it is time to reflect on what might lie beneath. To do this, we stay with the emotional experience, treating it kindly and leaning in with curiosity. Usually, as we put the pieces of our experience together, a pattern or a beautiful logic starts to appear, such as *"Oh I get angry and lash out when I really feel hurt or scared"* or *"I feel angry and vengeful thinking about my partner moving on happily, while underneath I am scared that I won't find love again."* So, try to reflect on your experience (it's OK if this feels uncomfortable, my aim is to help you, not judge you):

- *Are your angry feelings gushing out in a vain hope of reconnection with your lost love?*

- *Is your anger an attempt to make contact and be heard?*
- *Is it an attempt to punish the other for being hurtful or abandoning?*
- *Is it protesting the loss and your hurt?*
- *Is it born of injustice that this should never have happened?*

I find it helpful to look for the *protest*, the *pain* and the *protection* in the angry reaction. As an experienced Clinical Psychologist in the field of relationship therapy, **I have never met an angry reaction, no matter how aversive or illogical on the surface, that does not have pain at its core, an attachment protest embedded in it, and a protective function.**

Ask yourself:

- *What is your anger protecting you from?*
- *What is the pain that is embedded in it?*
- *What is the essence of the protest in your anger?*

Even if angry feelings have vengeful elements, like secretly hoping your ex-partner meets with a nasty accident or their new partner contracts terminal halitosis, we want to acknowledge the more tender emotions that are underneath. These are the primary emotions, and they can be obvious or elusive. There may be hurt over rejection, fear of being unlovable, or sadness about the loss of what could have been underneath these reactive expressions.

Another way to find the function in the anger is to ask yourself the following questions:

- *How would you feel or what would it mean to you if that anger was heard and acknowledged?*
- *If that terrible thing happened to your ex-partner, what would that give you?*
- *If that pain, that need, that longing was attended to, what would that free you from? What wound in you would that soothe?*

We are not trying to talk ourselves out of the reaction here or to challenge it; we are genuinely connecting with our emotional experience to find the heart of what is most painful. When we find the pain, we find the attachment meaning in the anger, and when we find this, we are right next door to the primary emotion.

Basement – Finding the wisdom

To venture down into the deepest level of your emotional world, I invite you to take the *function* of the anger (the protest, the pain, and the protection) and allow yourself to really feel into this, to stay with it, and to notice how you feel in your body as you let yourself connect with that pain.

- *What is most painful about this loss on a core level? What breaks your heart?*
- *What are you longing for, crying out for that you're not receiving?*
- *How do you feel inside as you let yourself touch into that experience?*
- *Can you make room for those most tender feelings? Can you be with them?*

When we can be with our pain and hold ourselves gently and without judgement, then the emotion can *do its work*. If we stay with it and allow it to be there and treat the part of us that hurts with loving kindness, then the emotion will begin to transform. It becomes easier to have, it unfolds like a beautiful flower and the meaning becomes clearer. We can now discover the wisdom in it that tells us what we want and need at our deepest level, and it can move us in the direction of what matters most to us. Again, ask yourself:

- *What are you most needing at a deep, core level?*
- *How is it for you to let yourself feel into this pain and this need?*
- *What are you learning about yourself and your needs that you hadn't experienced before?*
- *Do you need something from your ex-partner, or do you need to give something to yourself?*

Preventing stuckness

Now that you have had some practice (and it can take a bit of practice) with connecting with your deepest feelings and needs, you might be discovering that your reactivity is actually coming from hurt, sadness, fear, or shame. We are going to be looking at how to process these feelings and how to be a resource for yourself in Chapters 6 and 7. However, you might be realising that the reactive anger you have been feeling is coming from a deeper, primary sense of slow-burn anger because you have been betrayed or mistreated. This primary anger is telling you, rightly so, that an injustice has happened and that you need to stand your ground and fight to be heard or never to be hurt like that again. The sense of unfairness and lack of accountability for a hurtful act can certainly keep some people stuck in their anger. It is completely understandable that if you have been wronged, you need the wrongdoer to be held accountable and for them to witness the impact of their hurtful act. Sometimes, this can happen, and at other times, it cannot. When someone else holds the key to release you from your internal inferno and they are not willing or able to unlock it, then you are in a tough spot. We are going to look at how to work through this injustice and how to detach from a painful relationship in Chapter 6.

Chapter 4 takeaways

- We learn powerful lessons about anger in our earliest attachment relationships. These impact how we respond to and express anger.
- Bowlby acknowledged that anxiety and anger are normal reactions to an attachment figure's inexplicable absence.
- He defined the process of reactions to the loss of an attachment figure as numbing, yearning and searching (protest), disorganisation and despair, and reorganisation and detachment.
- In order to successfully adjust to the loss of an attachment figure, Bowlby argued that people need to reorganise their inner world in such a way that they no longer seek out the lost love as a safe haven of comfort or secure base for encouragement.
- Bowlby also said that angry reproach after a period of separation was a natural part of restoring the bond and ensuring that similar separations don't happen in future. This is adaptive if the bond can be repaired but it is not adaptive to keep searching and yearning and protesting when the bond cannot be repaired or restored.
- People with secure attachment strategies seem to be less likely to struggle emotionally after a breakup than those with insecure attachment strategies (anxious, avoidant, or fearful-avoidant attachment strategies).

- People with anxious attachment strategies are more likely to experience high distress, to become preoccupied with thoughts about the ex-partner, to seek contact with and attempt to re-establish the connection, to be angry and vengeful towards the ex-partner, and to keep turning to them for support.
- People with avoidant attachment strategies are more likely to display lower levels of emotional disturbance and to use self-reliant coping strategies but to blame themselves, to feel reluctant to date again, and to have diminished interest in sex, showing that the breakup impacts them internally despite looking unimpacted externally.
- There are only six to eight universal core, primary emotions and they are generally versions of joy, sadness, anger, fear, shame, and surprise.
- Primary emotion is the most important and meaningful type of emotion because it comes right from the heart of our emotional world and is embedded in rich meaning about what is most important to us.
- Reactive emotion is fast, it is intense, and it is on the surface. It often masks primary emotions and can cause damage to relationships.
- Being angry isn't an excuse for being aggressive, threatening, intimidating, coercive, or hurtful.
- People don't usually get angry without a reason. At the core of an angry reaction, there is always pain, an attachment protest, and a protective function. We just have to be able to slow it down and listen to find the wisdom in it about our deepest needs and fears, the primary emotions.
- Tune into your anger by noticing the trigger, the body sensations, the meaning you make, and what you usually do to manage it. Look for the function in your angry feelings, the deeper needs, and softer feelings beneath angry reactivity. Let these deeper needs guide your next steps into more productive action.

Notes

1. Sbarra, D. A., & Emery, R. E. (2005). The emotional sequelae of nonmarital relationship dissolution: Analysis of change and intraindividual variability over time. *Personal Relationships, 12*(2), 213–232.
2. Bowlby, J. (1979). *The making and breaking of affectional bonds.* London: Tavistock.

3. Fraley, R. C., & Shaver, P. R. (1999). Loss and bereavement: Attachment theory and recent controversies concerning "grief work" and the nature of detachment. In J. Cassidy & P. R. Shaver (Eds.), *Handbook of attachment: Theory, research, and clinical applications* (pp. 735–759). New York: Guilford.

4. Bowlby, J., & Parkes, C. M. (1970). Separation and loss within the family. In E. J. Anthony & C. Koupernik (Eds.), *The child in his family: International yearbook of child psychiatry and allied professionals* (pp. 197–216). New York: Wiley.

5. Bowlby, J. (1980). *Attachment and loss: Volume 3. Loss: Sadness and depression.* New York: Basic Books.

6. Sbarra, D. A. (2006). Predicting the onset of emotional recovery following nonmarital relationship dissolution: A survival analyses of sadness and anger. *Personality and Social Psychology Bulletin, 32*(3), 298–312.

7. Madey, S. F., & Jilek, L. (2012). Attachment style and dissolution of romantic relationships: Breaking up is hard to do, or is it? *Individual Differences Research, 10*(4), 202–210.

8. Davis, D., Shaver, P. R., & Vernon, M. L. (2003). Physical, emotional and behavioural reactions to breaking up: The roles of gender, age, emotional involvement, and attachment style. *Personality & Social Psychology Bulletin, 29*(7), 871–884.

9. Marshall, T. C., Bejanyan, K., & Ferenczi, N. (2013). Attachment styles and personal growth following romantic breakups: The mediating roles of distress, rumination, and tendency to rebound. *PLOS ONE, 8*(9), e75161.

10. Fagundes, C. P. (2012). Getting over you: Contributions of attachment theory for post-breakup emotional adjustment. *Personal Relationships, 19*(1), 37–50.

11. Birnbaum, G. E., Orr, I., Mikulincer, M., & Florian, V. (1997). When marriage breaks up: Does attachment style contribute to coping and mental health? *Journal of Social and Personal Relationships, 14*(5), 643–654.

12. Furrow, J., Johnson, S., Bradley, B., Brubacher, L., Campbell, L., Kallos-Lilly, V., Palmer, G., Rheem, K., & Woolley, S. (in press). *Becoming an emotionally focused couple therapist: The workbook* (2nd ed.). New York: Routledge.

13. Bowlby, J. (1973). *Attachment & loss: Volume 2. Separation: Anxiety and anger.* London: Tavistock.

14. Frijda, N. H. (1986). *The Emotions.* Cambridge, England: Cambridge University Press.

15. Davis, K. L., & Montag, C. (2019). Selected principles of Pankseppian affective neuroscience. *Frontiers in Neuroscience, 12*, 1025.

16. Johnson, S. M. (2019). *Attachment theory in practice: Emotionally focused therapy (EFT) with individuals, couples and families.* New York: The Guilford Press.

FIVE

Grief and attachment

In Chapter 4, we looked at separation and loss from an attachment perspective and delved into the turbulent waters of anger. Now that we can see our anger, fear, and sadness as a natural expression of the absence of someone special to you, it makes sense that these emotions move you in the direction of attempting to recover the bond, even when it can no longer be saved. Bowlby described our predictable reactions to loss as numbing, yearning and searching (protest), disorganisation and despair, and reorganisation and detachment.[1] While Chapter 4 focused on the yearning and searching phase, this chapter will focus on the disorganisation and despair phase. We will explore what it means to confront the reality of the loss, to give up searching and fighting to recover the bond, and to plunge headlong into the despair of knowing it cannot be recovered, that it is forever altered. This is pretty rocky territory, but remember you're not alone, this book will guide you.

In this chapter, we are going to dive deeply into the grief of loss. We will be naming, owning, and making room for the ruthless pain that accompanies the loss of an important relationship. We will look at what we can learn from the research on the emotional impact of loss and how our attachment strategies play a role in both distress and in recovery from a lost attachment bond. We will explore and process the big, painful feelings that might be there for you, and will find what you are needing at your core to help you in your adjustment. This involves not only acknowledging the loss of someone special and all that this relationship could have been (this is extremely difficult for many), but also acknowledging the things that might have been missing for you, your unmet attachment needs (also very difficult). We will explore how you can be there for yourself and reach out to others in these most desperately harrowing moments. We will

DOI: 10.4324/9781003264163-8

find a pathway into and through the grief and look at some strategies for riding the waves of emotion until the storm starts to pass, which although hard to believe now, it will.

Attachment-focused view of grief

The loss of an important relationship is, in many ways, like a death. I have heard many despairing and heartbroken people say to me through tears and with extreme hesitancy and terrible guilt that it would be easier for them if their partner had actually died. While they felt awful for thinking in this way, it makes sense from an attachment perspective. The loss of an attachment bond is extremely painful, regardless of how it happens. When we have lost someone special through the dissolution or reconfiguring of a relationship, the loss can be excruciating. If your partner lives on but no longer chooses you, the combination of loss and rejection can be unbearable. If you have made the gut-wrenching decision to end a relationship, knowing that you are inflicting pain on someone you care about, this is a painful mix of guilt *and* loss. Even when both partners make a mutual decision to end or redefine their relationship, despite trying really hard to make it work, the pain and helplessness can be overwhelming. When a bond is snapped beyond repair by an act of betrayal, then the loss is compounded by broken promises and agonising hurt. If you are the one who broke the trust, then the self-reproach in combination with the loss can be monumental. Whichever way you have come upon your loss and pain, I know that it will be creating its own brand of suffering – we need to make space for this to be heard, acknowledged, and learned from. I am here to both make sense of this and to hopefully cushion the suffering through unconditional understanding.

Researchers have proposed that the emotional experience following the end of a relationship is akin to the grief following the death of partner. A critical difference, however, is that unlike death, the loss of a relationship is theoretically reversible, which can make the grieving more complicated.[2] Managing the emotional storms within yourself can be extremely difficult after the loss of an attachment figure. Bowlby said that the loss of a loved one is one of the most intensely painful experiences any human being can suffer, and that to the grieving person, nothing can bring comfort other than the return of the lost person. He also said that there is a tendency to underestimate how intensely distressing and disabling the loss usually is and the length of time it can take to recover.[3] Grieving partners can continue to pine for their ex-partners long after separation, sometimes for years, and they are particularly sensitive to reminders of their lost love. As a result, they can struggle to process and adjust to the loss or to imagine any future, especially with a new partner.[4] Remember, it hurts because it matters, and your pain honours the love you felt, and indeed may still feel, for this special person. If you are willing to open your heart to love, then you risk bravely. Your risk has left you hurt this time, but it won't always hurt this much, and you will find love again – but first, we need to help your poor, sore heart to heal.

As discussed in the last chapter, we have come to understand that anger and fear are normal reactions to being separated from a loved one. Bowlby described this as the *yearning and searching* (protest) phase of grief. As humans, we seem to universally react with fear and anger to separation from our attachment figure, even when we know that the bond cannot be repaired and that the other is not coming back to us. These galvanising emotions release energy that is thrown into restoring the bond, *which is adaptive when the bond can be restored and maladaptive when it cannot.* When a person becomes stuck in this phase or their reactive anger becomes threatening to another, this can be harmful to all involved. We looked at ways to work through reactive anger to access the softer, primary emotions underneath that provide vital information about a person's longings and fears and deepest needs. Once someone has done the painful work of understanding their angry feelings and reframed them as protest and searching in vain for the lost love, a brutal realisation on a heart-level that the other is lost to them is likely to hit them. This is when people are expected to collapse into the next phase of the grief process according to Bowlby, which is *disorganisation and despair*. In this phase, the true reality of the loss is encountered, hope recedes, and a person's world is turned upside down. It takes considerable work to move through this phase to the final phase of *reorganisation and detachment*.[5] You may find yourself in or entering this phase as you read this book. You are human, as am I, so despite these feelings, please know you are not alone in exploring them.

Bowlby's phases of grief overlap quite well with recent developments in the field of grief and loss that reject the idea of grief being a linear process, preferring to see the process of grief as involving four key tasks. This is an empowering and active view of grief that bestows agency upon the griever to achieve these four tasks: acceptance of the reality of the loss, experiencing the pain of the loss, adjusting to life without the lost love, and finding a connection to the past without becoming stuck in it.[6] Bowlby's phases align well with these four tasks of grief. While models like this can orientate us, it is important to recognise that grief is not a straightforward process. It is an emotional and organic process that evolves and shifts. People's experience of grief will vary greatly in terms of how long they might remain in each phase and their movement back and forth between phases. You may experience periods of animated protest against the separation and make attempts to contact your ex-partner for resolution and then sink into despair at other moments, crying and unmotivated to face the world. You will have good days where you can attend to the functional aspects of life and glimpse some hope for the future, and you will have bad days where you are consumed with the injustice or the despair of the loss and wonder how you will ever go on. Overall, the hope is that you will gradually move *forward* as you process your feelings and make sense of the loss. We are going to look at how to do this in more detail, so let's start by focusing a bit more on what happens inside when we are thrown into disorganisation and despair. I know this is really difficult, so try to hang in there.

As you know, separation from an attachment figure is stressful and disorganising to our emotional world. The loss of our safe haven of comfort and secure base of support is devastating to humans. It's no wonder that once we accept that no amount of protesting will bring our special other back and we can accept the reality of the loss, it is disorganising for us. Not only is loss emotionally painful, it turns our world upside down. You are not just grieving the loss of your special person; you are grieving the lost fabric of your life. Of course, how much your world becomes upended by this loss depends on the nature of the lost relationship and whether you were prepared or unprepared for the end of the relationship.

It is understandable that distress and disorganisation is most acute for those who were unprepared for the loss, who did not end the relationship, and who had limited knowledge of problems in the partnership.[7] If this is your situation and you were completely blindsided by this loss, then you are likely to be scrambling to take in not only the loss of the person but also your entire life as you knew it. Shared plans for the future and the imagined life that you and your partner envisaged and banked on are now all forever altered. You are probably grieving not just for the happy memories, but for the memories you hadn't even made yet, and for the moments that hadn't happened and now never will. It can cause you to look back at the relationship with new eyes and to question those happy memories and your version of reality. It can make you re-write history and doubt your perception of moments you shared together. Loss can completely upend a person's view of their past and of their future. Suddenly, everything you thought you knew might be in question and you might feel that you have no map forwards, you can even find yourself asking who you are, where you are going, whether you are to blame for this loss, and even whether you are fundamentally unlovable. This loss leaves an aching void, where it can feel like there is no safe other to turn to for co-regulation, no ally to stand shoulder-to-shoulder with as you face the world, and an awful feeling of isolation.

If this loss was a little more expected or if you were the one to make the decision to end the relationship, then you may have had more time to reconcile this loss. This can mean that the distress and disorganisation is less acute because the road to this place is likely to have been long, and you have had time to make sense of this change to your life. However, I'm sure that the decision to end the relationship won't have come easily and, even if you can see that the relationship was not benefiting anyone, the reality of its ending can bring back many of the struggles mentioned so far. There may be doubts about whether you have made the right decision, guilt about hurting the other and worry for your ex-partner's well-being. If you are not proud of things you have done during the relationship or to bring about its demise, then this can be an additional heavy burden for you to carry, which can alter your view of yourself and create another element of disorganisation to your experience. In this way, you are both handling a loss and being burdened by responsibility for causing harm to someone you care deeply about. That is a really hard place to be.

In this way, the process of grief encompasses not only the loss of the other, but also the loss of the hopes and dreams for the shared future you imagined together. Your experience may include self-doubt or even the loss of your own identity – it can rob a person of the hope of ever finding love again and can create a fear of even trying. All in all, it is vicious and unrelenting. You can feel caught between a past that is too full of feelings and a future that seems deprived of feelings. Making room for the intricacy of your own personal experience is an important part of the work of grief.

Processing your grief

Relationship loss shares a common set of challenges, and these are *interpersonal*, as in how you negotiate your ongoing relationship with your-ex partner and your life without them, and *intrapersonal*, as in how you manage the grief and loss within yourself. We can see that "successful grief" is an ability to accept and adapt to the loss of someone special so that you might be able to move on with your life, perhaps even stronger for the experience of that connection. Bowlby defined healthy grieving as the successful effort to accept both that a change has occurred in our external world and that we are required to make corresponding changes to our internal, representational world and to reorganise, and perhaps reorientate, our attachment behaviour accordingly. This means that we have to be able to process the pain of the loss and redefine our loved-one in our mind as no longer being the one we turn to when life gets bumpy. In effect, you are *undoing* your attachment bond with that person. As good as it might have felt creating that bond, the undoing is as excruciatingly painful. A crucial part of this process involves confronting the reality of the loss. However, this can be very challenging because of the intensity of the emotions involved. Accepting that you have lost someone special to you brings with it an awful sadness that can be seen as a withdrawal state; a place into which you retreat once it is crystal clear that there can be no reunion. Only from this place can you re-evaluate the relationship, make room for the pain, and look at moving forward in a new way.

How people do this and how they might become stuck in this process is impacted by many things, including the attachment strategies they tend to use. We know from our earlier explorations into this topic in Chapter 4 that those with secure attachment strategies are more likely to regulate their emotions, to seek support from others, and to move more smoothly through the process of grieving a lost relationship than those who use insecure attachment strategies (anxious, avoidant, or fearful-avoidant).

Those with *anxious* attachment strategies are more likely to be tuned into their partner's availability and to be sensitive to cues of possible rejection; therefore, the loss of an attachment figure is experienced as extremely distressing. Following the end of a relationship, people with anxious attachment strategies are more likely to become preoccupied with thoughts of their ex-partner, to make attempts to repair or reconcile, and to continue to use their ex-partner as a source of support. These tendencies seem to play a role in slowing the adjustment process. Conversely, those who use *avoidant* attachment strategies might be more at risk of speeding through the grieving process and not processing the loss enough. This might be because avoidant attachment strategies often involve emotional distancing from themselves and their partner, and so they might not form as deep an emotional connection, which could leave them either less emotionally impacted by their loss or less aware of the emotional impact of the loss on their emotional world.[8]

It is worth noting that the research on the impact of attachment strategies on post-relationship adjustment seems to be limited to looking only at secure, anxious, and avoidant attachment strategies. Fearful-avoidant attachment strategies are not exclusively explored, possibly because these attachment strategies incorporate features of anxious pursuit for connection and avoidant withdrawal from closeness for fear of being hurt. Despite this, we can expect that in grief and loss, people with fearful-avoidant attachment strategies might experience both anxious distress at the loss and withdrawal from the ex-partner in oscillating amounts. If you identify with these attachment strategies, take a moment to notice which mode (as in anxious pursuit or avoidance) might be more dominant for you in your grieving.

Coping with a loss of this magnitude involves working through the loss to extract the meaning in it *and* managing the emotional pain and dysregulation to restore everyday functioning. This involves two important emotional processes at once, turning up the heat in some areas, and turning down the heat in others. To illustrate this, it helps to think of the "work" of grief as involving two important tasks.[9] The first is the *emotional* work of processing the loss. This includes thinking about the lost partner, yearning for them, reflecting on the relationship and how it ended, remembering the good times, and learning from the not-so-good times, and being with the pain of the loss. Emotional work of this nature is taxing, and no one can do this exclusively. People need to be able to come up for air or they would become overwhelmed by their emotional pain, and they would not be able to function. That said, not all the emotional work of processing a loss might be negative. There may be moments of positivity in reflecting on pleasant memories or moments of relief and hope for the future.

The other equally important task of grieving is the *practical* work of coping with day-to-day life and adjusting the practical aspects of your life to the loss. This might involve making decisions about living arrangements, changes to finances, managing co-parenting of any children, changing employment status, or the building of new social connections. As you can see, this is quite a distinct process compared to the emotional work of processing the loss, but that does not mean that there is not an emotional element to these life decisions and adjustments. In this way, both the emotional and the practical tasks of grieving are equally important to a person's progress in adjusting to the separation from their special person. Healthy grief is thought to balance these two tasks and to move flexibly between them so that emotions can be attended to, and life-transitioning can be accomplished. Cultural context is important as well; cultural belief systems teach us about how grief is manifested and expressed, and this must be respected as well. All reactions are okay, and all are important. Emotions may come and go, arising and disappearing unexpectedly, and a person's ability to face the practical challenges without their ex-partner might also come and go. Attending to both tasks, the emotional and practical, is vital to the recovery process.

This model is called the *Dual Process Model of Coping with Bereavement* and I appreciate the equal value it places on all ways of grieving without favouring one style more than another. It acknowledges that no one can be in the thick of their emotional experience all the time, and also that it is not altogether healthy to be solely focused on the practicalities of the loss either. This model is realistic in highlighting that we will move in and out of either task, sometimes we are making really adaptive practical decisions, when suddenly we are plunged into our emotions and are in floods of tears. At other times, we are so organised and efficient in our problem solving that people marvel at how well we are coping, but then we are awake all night thinking about our lost love. Sometimes we need to emotionally free-wheel and allow for some distraction from the "heavy-duty work" of grief. At other times, we might be able to laugh at happy memories only to be heartbroken by a cute puppy video or by witnessing another loving relationship. As we alluded to earlier, **if you are processing emotion, focusing on practicalities, and allowing yourself to breathe, then no matter how messy and disorganised it might appear, you are doing the work needed to successfully navigate this loss.**

I must offer a note of caution here by saying that it is important that you keep an eye on *both* the emotional and the practical tasks of grieving so that neither area is neglected. We know that becoming engulfed in painful emotion for extended periods of time is going to impact a person's ability to function in life and we know that suppressing painful emotions is effortful and wearing on a person's well-being.[10] So long as you can turn up the heat if you notice a reluctance in either task or turn down the heat if either task is becoming too much, then you are flexibly meeting the challenge of grief. You could call this "Goldilocks flexibility." For instance, someone with avoidant attachment strategies might naturally find themselves turning to the practical tasks of making life-adjustments and moving away from the emotional tasks required to process the loss. They might need to turn up the heat on their emotional processing of the loss and really tune into their sad feelings to be sure that they are honoured. Someone with anxious attachment strategies might naturally do the emotional work of grieving but feel out of their depth in navigating the practical adjustments they need to make to move forwards from the loss. They might need to work to turn down the heat on their emotional reactions and allocate some time for focusing on the practical arrangements that need to be made to ready themselves for the next phase of their life. This explains Bowlby's observations that people struggle in their acceptance of a loss if they either move too quickly through the phases of grief or if they become arrested in either the protest or despair phase. I want to help you to be self-aware so that you can ensure that both tasks of grief have equal airplay. Of course, this is all the harder, unlike other life tasks, because it is your special attachment figure who might have helped you to do this, and they are no longer there to be turned to as a resource. That said, I urge you to muster others in your life to help you in this process wherever you can. This is hard work to do all on your own, and remember, we work best when we can co-regulate with a safe other. If this can't be your ex-partner, think of who else in your world you could pull close to be of help in your grief.

Let's take a moment to reflect on your own approach to your loss.

- *Which "task" of grief (emotional or practical) do you naturally find easier and why?*
- *Which do you find more difficult and why?*
- *How does this correspond with your most commonly used attachment strategies?*
- *What do you need to do to make sure that you can tune in more to the task you tend to neglect?*
- *Who could help you with this?*

Managing "too much" or "not enough" emotional contact

Seeing that helping you to manage the practical adjustments that you need to make in your life is probably not in my wheelhouse, I feel that I can probably be of more use in helping you navigate the emotional work of grief.

It appears that people differ in what feels like a healthy or unhealthy amount of reflection on their feelings about the loss of an attachment figure. While we know that attending to the emotions that are activated by a loss is an important task in the work of grief, there is some evidence that intensive processing of your thoughts and feelings about a loss might actually be counterproductive, if you tend to use anxious attachment strategies, but not if you tend to use avoidant attachment strategies. This is because people who use anxious attachment strategies are more likely to feel higher levels of post-breakup distress and to be more sensitive to rejection and abandonment themes. As a result, they can find it difficult to turn down the heat on their negative emotions and often intensify their emotions compared to people who don't use anxious attachment strategies.[11] This means that they might focus on the negative themes of the loss, perhaps to their own detriment.[12] However, the potential silver lining in experiencing high levels of distress post-breakup is that it could be associated with more personal growth such as making positive life changes in response to negative life events. In other words, we can learn to cope better, especially when we are informed and self-reflective.

Even though experiencing high levels of distress is no picnic, it seems that the pain of a relationship loss has the potential to exert a transformational effect. The implication here is that people who use avoidant attachment strategies, while experiencing less distress after a loss, might be missing an opportunity for the personal growth that is inherent in the suffering and reflection that accompanies a loss.[13] This is pretty amazing because it shows that the emotional work of processing the uncomfortable feelings in relation to a relationship loss actually can be instrumental in adjustment to the loss and to further personal growth after the fact. However, it seems that how a person interacts with their post-loss raw feelings can determine whether they become stuck in their negative feelings or whether they move through them to achieve growth.

Another important aspect of the emotional processing of a loss that we need to attend to is whether you find yourself turning to your ex-partner in the hope of a positive response to your bids for contact. Many people who use anxious attachment strategies can fall into this pattern of amplifying their signals of need in the hope that their ex-partner will respond in a caring and engaged manner. This means that they can exert considerable energy into seeking out their ex-partner, which only causes them more upset and rejection if their partner does not respond positively. This thwarted attempt at reconnection can serve to prolong the recovery process by "picking at the scab" that was just starting to form a crust. If you find yourself tempted to contact your ex-partner in the hope of receiving some care or understanding, please remember that this could be slowing your recovery. If this is a habit that you have fallen into, then changing who you reach out to for support is one practical step you can take to help your recovery along its path.

We are learning that reflection on the emotional fall-out of a relationship loss might be helpful, but *how* this reflection happens might be the key to whether it is a help or a hindrance to healing. We can see that for people with anxious attachment strategies, who tend to experience their emotions more strongly, reflecting on their feelings about a loss can become a hindrance to their recovery if they remain stuck in the negative themes and repeat unhelpful patterns from the past, but it can help them to grow if they process their pain and move through it in new ways. However, for those who use avoidant attachment strategies, and therefore are not as in tune with their emotional world, by not tuning into the emotional pain of their loss, they might miss an important opportunity for self-growth. For them, paying more attention to their feelings post-breakup could potentially be a helpful part of their recovery. Taken together, it is clear that you need to know your own attachment strategies and be aware of how you are interacting (or not) with your emotional world. Sounds so simple, doesn't it? Let's read on together.

Getting the balance right

Taken in balance, we are discovering that spending time with your emotions and reflecting on the pain of a loss can be helpful *if* this contact allows you to process the loss in a productive way that leads to self-awareness and self-growth. Spending time with your painful emotions is unhelpful if you experience them as overwhelming, and they keep you stuck in an endless loop of unproductive pain, which leads to unsuccessful attempts to be soothed and repeated rejections from others. Being aware of your own attachment strategies and whether your own emotional processing is helping or hindering your recovery is vital to being able to recover in the most meaningful and efficient way. No one wants to be hurting a moment longer than they need, but not hurting enough can mean that you miss an opportunity for self-knowledge and personal growth. Let's start by looking at how to manage emotions that feel "too much" and then look at how to work with experiences that are "not enough" emotionally.

If you are concerned that the intensity of your emotional reaction to the loss of your partner is too high and that it could be causing you harm and preventing you from focusing on some of the more practical elements of your grief work, then let's look at how to manage this more effectively. It is clear that processing your painful emotions is part of the work of grief. However, if the intensity of your emotions is too high or if you find yourself engaging in self-defeating behaviours in an attempt to alleviate them, then this is going to stall your recovery. In contrast, if you can utilise yourself or others as supports in a way that allows you to redirect your attachment needs away from your ex-partner, then this is going to set you on a different path. If you can connect with your vulnerable emotions in a loving and open way that honours your own pain, it will allow you to make sense of this loss and to create a new way forward for yourself – that is the most adaptive and empowering use of your emotions of all. No wonder there is the capacity for personal growth.

Despite these benefits, it is important to keep your feelings about this loss within a workable window of tolerance.[14] This window needs to be open wide enough that you are able to make contact with your painful feelings in order to process the loss adaptively. This means being able to engage with your experience, to tune into your needs, and best figure out how to move forwards, while informed by the wisdom of your emotional world. However, the window needs to not be so wide that all feelings engulf you and throw you off balance – reeling into old ways of coping that you know are not good for you. Remember, "Goldilocks flexibility." This is somewhat of an art form. If you struggle with turning down the intensity of your big feelings about this loss – to narrow the window – then you need some tools in your tool kit.

Some people in this situation like to write their feelings down so that they seem more manageable; others like to allow themselves a period of time for ruminating on the loss and then distracting themselves with something pleasant and absorbing to mark the end of that allotted time. Other people like to use the support of a good and honest friend who can tell them if they are disappearing down the rabbit hole into dysfunctional places. Managing your self-care by eating well, getting enough sleep, and taking regular exercise will all resource you and improve your sense of resilience. Arming yourself with a practical plan of action for the next few months can also provide structure, and drawing upon the more practical tasks of grieving can help you see some light at the end of the tunnel. Mindfulness and grounding techniques are very useful for regulating intense emotion. They can either become part of a daily habit to reduce baseline levels of stress, or they can be used in an intense moment to help you to remain present, while at a working distance from your strong emotions. I generally recommend that people make this part of a daily practise, so that they are skilled up, and have strengthened the "muscle" of their attention to be able to direct it where they choose in these escalated moments. Attuning to the deeper need embedded in your distress is also very important to making sense of the function in emotional reactivity and accessing the wisdom of underlying primary emotions. We touched on this in Chapter 4, and we are going to revisit this process next.

Tuning into your emotional world

If you struggle with making contact with your inner emotional world and tend to remain practical, or if you are only comfortable with certain emotions but shy away from the vulnerable, painful emotions born of grief, then we need to look at how to tune into your inner world more completely. Firstly, having the intent to lean into your emotions with curiosity and openness is the starting point. Making a commitment to yourself to attend to your inner world by consciously tuning in regularly throughout the day can really help to operationalise this process. You might like to set a timer and to regularly check-in throughout the day, by pausing and asking yourself how you are feeling inside, noticing your body sensations, and assessing your emotional state. Having a little chart with general emotions listed on it can be helpful if you find it tricky to describe your feelings when they are not overly intense. Recording your emotion in a mood diary and jotting down any notes that relate to this feeing can be helpful as well (e.g., *I am feeling flat this morning because it is cloudy, and I know I have a lot to face today*). This will build your ability to notice and tune into your emotional world rather than dismissing it and getting on with the practicalities of life. A bit like putting a snorkel on and looking under the sea, you will be surprised at the richness of what you find there.

The ability to be with yourself in moments of vulnerability and pain is a lifelong skill that will only benefit your long-term self-growth. Tuning in with yourself like this is an important skill even for those who feel their emotions strongly, because sometimes the reactive emotions can take up all the space and prevent the really meaningful parts of our experience from being heard. If you recall us talking about reactive and primary emotions in Chapter 4, let's revisit this through the lens of grief and loss.

To go on this journey into your inner world, imagine you are taking the elevator from the top down into your inner emotional experience, level by level until we get to the basement or deepest levels of your emotional world. We are going to start with the sad, hurt, painful feelings that flare when you think about the loss of your relationship (reactive feelings). We are going to stay at the top level initially. These reactive emotions are considered first to make sense of them. Next, we are going to travel beneath them to find the richest source of meaning, your core or primary emotions that tell us about your deepest fears, longings, and needs.

Top floor – Noticing and attending

Firstly, we need to slow down and connect with these reactive feelings, knowing that there is something important for us to attend to in them.

To do this, ask yourself:

- *When does the pain of your loss come alive? What seems to <u>trigger</u> these feelings?*
- *What sensations do you notice in your <u>body</u> (and where) when these feelings flare?*
- *What do you tell yourself as you are feeling these most tender painful feelings? What is the <u>meaning</u> you are making about the situation, your ex-partner or yourself?*

Then notice how you tend to manage these feelings, or what action they predictably lead to.

- *What do you typically <u>do</u> to manage the intensity of these feelings? What actions are you driven to take when you feel this way?*

As you assemble the pieces of this experience, by exploring in this way, we know that big feelings become more ordered, clearer, and a little easier to have.

Ground floor – Finding the function

Now that you have assembled the fragments of your reactive or surface emotional experience, it is time to reflect on what might lie beneath. To do this, we stay with the emotional experience, treating it kindly and leaning in with curiosity. Usually, as we put the pieces of our experience together, a pattern or a beautiful logic starts to appear, such as, "*Oh I busy myself with work to avoid feeling sad about the loss*" or "*I'm afraid to touch into this loss because I think it will overwhelm me.*"

So, to reflect on your experience:

- *Are your sad feelings about the loss of your partner, or about your view of your future, or about your own self-blame? Or something else?*
- *Is your pain an attempt to make contact and be heard?*

We want to acknowledge the more tender emotions that are underneath those we might encounter on the surface. These are the primary emotions, and they can be obvious or elusive. When we really find and understand them, it can be literally a "light bulb" moment. This is part of our growth.

Basement – Finding the wisdom

To venture down into the deepest level of your emotional world can be painful. But, we are together, so I invite you to really feel into your sadness, to stay with it, and to notice how you feel in your body as you let yourself connect with that pain.

- *What is most painful about this loss on a core level? What breaks your heart?*
- *What are you longing for, crying out for that you're not receiving?*
- *How do you feel inside as you let yourself touch into that experience?*
- *Can you make room for those most tender feelings?*

When we can be with our pain and hold ourselves gently and without judgement, then the emotion can do its work. If we stay with it and allow it to be there and treat the part of us that hurts with loving kindness, then the emotion will begin to transform. It becomes easier to be with – it unfolds like a beautiful flower and the meaning becomes clearer. We can now discover the wisdom in it that tells us what we want and need at our deepest levels, and it can move us in the direction of what matters most to us.

- *What are you most needing at a deep, core level?*
- *How is it for you to let yourself feel into this pain and this need?*
- *What are you learning about yourself and your needs that you hadn't experienced before?*
- *Do you need something from your ex-partner, or do you need to give something to yourself?*

This work is so hard, but it is also so meaningful. You are learning to be with yourself in loving kindness and I know that that can only take you to wonderful places. Confrontation with the reality of the loss is crucial to adaptive grieving, and it needs to be done in a way that honours the individual, the lost relationship, and the cultural context. The work of grief cannot be done relentlessly, it needs to be "dosed" in a way that feels manageable. In other words, it does take time. Moving flexibly between touching into the emotional significance of the loss as well as attending to the practical life-adjustments required are both valid components of the work of grief. Please be kind to yourself and respect your own emotional process as you move through these phases of grieving in your own perfectly imperfect way. Be sure to tune into your inner world to tap into the remarkable wisdom there. In Chapter 6, we are going to look at taking the learnings from the loss of this relationship into the future. We are going to look at letting go, at forgiving yourself and your ex-partner, at releasing yourself from this past, and at moving forward into a brighter future.

When to seek professional help

If you find yourself regularly engulfed in the painful emotions of grief and loss and have days when you cannot get out of bed that stretch into a full week or more, or where you seriously consider that it would be better to not be alive, then I am concerned that you might need more support in your recovery. You might not be able to heal from this relational loss alone, and you might need the help of a professional with skills in assisting you in this process. Relational pain requires loving relationships with safe others to help you through it. We all need safe others to help us, and sometimes this group of supporters needs to include a professional as well. You aren't alone if you need this, and it can vastly assist in your recovery. The more supporters you have, the better.

Chapter 5 takeaways

- Separation from an attachment figure is distressing and painful. Once the reality of the loss is accepted and you are no longer searching and yearning in an attempt to recover the lost bond, then you are likely to experience despair and disorganisation, which can be extremely destabilising.
- Disorganisation is a state of awareness that your entire world, past, present, and future, is upended by this loss.
- The "work" of grief involves attending to two important tasks, the *practical* elements of adjusting to life without your relationship as you knew it, and the *emotional* work of processing the meaning of the loss.
- Being aware of your own attachment strategies and your natural proclivity to either the *practical* or the *emotional* task of grieving is important in making sure that neither area is neglected.

- Knowing how to work within your own emotional window of tolerance is vital to being able to tune into your emotional world enough to learn from it and to grow, without becoming flooded by your emotions, and sending you back into old patterns of coping.
- Accepting the reality of the loss is crucial to adaptive grieving, and it needs to be done in a gradual way that honours the individual, the lost relationship, and the cultural context.
- If you are processing emotion, focusing on practicalities, and allowing yourself to breathe, then no matter how messy and disorganised it might appear, you are doing the work needed to successfully navigate this loss.
- Help is available if you need more support in this process; grieving cannot be done alone.

Notes

1. Bowlby, J. (1979). *The making and breaking of affectional bonds.* London: Tavistock.
2. Sbarra, D. A., & Emery, R. E. (2005). The emotional sequelae of nonmarital relationship dissolution: Analysis of change and intraindividual variability over time. *Personal Relationships, 12*(2), 213–232.
3. Bowlby, J. (1980). *Attachment and loss: Volume 3. Loss: Sadness and depression.* New York: Basic Books.
4. Fraley, R. C., & Shaver, P. R. (2000). Adult romantic attachment: Theoretical developments, emerging controversies, and unanswered questions. *Review of General Psychology, 4*(2), 132–154.
5. Bowlby, J., & Parkes, C. M. (1970). Separation and loss within the family. In E. J. Anthony & C. Koupernik (Eds.), *The child in his family: International yearbook of child psychiatry and allied professionals* (pp. 197–216). New York: Wiley.
6. Worden, W. J. (2018). *Grief counselling and grief therapy, 5th Edition: A handbook for the mental health professional.* New York, NY: Springer.
7. Fagundes, C. P. (2012). Getting over you: Contributions of attachment theory for post-breakup emotional adjustment. *Personal Relationships, 19*(1), 37–50.
8. Davis, D., Shaver, P. R., & Vernon, M. L. (2003). Physical, emotional and behavioural reactions to breaking up: The roles of gender, age, emotional involvement, and attachment style. *Personality & Social Psychology Bulletin, 29*(7), 871–884.
9. Stroebe, M., & Schut, H. (1999). The dual process model of coping with bereavement: Rationale and description. *Death Studies, 23*(3), 197–224.

10. Gross, J. J., & Levenson, R. W. (1997). Hiding feelings: The acute effects of inhibited negative and positive emotion. *Journal of Abnormal Psychology, 106*(1), 95–103.

11. Shaver, P. R., & Mikulincer, M. (2016). *Attachment in adulthood: Structure, dynamics and change* (2nd ed.). New York: The Guilford Press.

12. Nolen-Hoeksema, S., Parker, L. E., & Larson, J. (1994). Ruminative coping with depressed mood following loss. *Journal of Personality and Social Psychology, 67*(1), 92–104.

13. Marshall, T. C., Bejanyan, K., & Ferenczi, N. (2013). Attachment styles and personal growth following romantic breakups: The mediating roles of distress, rumination, and tendency to rebound. *PLOS ONE, 8*(9), e75161.

14. Siegel, D. J. (1999). *The developing mind*. New York: The Guilford Press.

PART III

Looking forward –
What's next for me?

SIX

Acceptance and detaching

As we have seen, Bowlby described the predictable reactions to relationship loss as numbing, yearning and searching (protest), disorganisation and despair, and reorganisation and detachment.[1] So far in our journey together, we have looked at the attachment view on separation and loss, and we have delved into the turbulent waters of anger as we explored the *searching and yearning* (protest) phase (Chapter 4). Then, we looked at how loss is not only sad, but how it turns your whole life upside down, as we investigated the *disorganisation and despair* phase (Chapter 5). We have come to see that anger, fear, and sadness are all part of the natural expression of losing someone special to you – it makes sense that these emotions move you in the direction of initially attempting to recover the bond, but then sinking into desolation once the reality of the loss is fully realised. We have looked at what is involved in the "work" of grieving a loss as important as this one. As we continue to map and track our way through these four phases of grief, we find ourselves now at the final phase – *reorganisation and detachment*.

In this chapter, we are going to spend time exploring this final phase in the process of grief and loss. This is the final piece of the puzzle where all the hurt and anguish can come together to create a coherent narrative of what went wrong and why. It is where you can reconcile the pain, regret, guilt, fear, and sadness, and can let go. We will find ways for you to forgive yourself and others, where needed, and to reconcile what has happened in a way that builds your resilience. We will focus on detaching your attachment energies from your ex-partner and on shifting and building your support system to maximise your positive connections with those who nourish you and lift you up. This will allow you to move forwards in your life, with greater self-awareness and self-compassion. You will find that you can be healed and whole again.

DOI: 10.4324/9781003264163-10

When life hands you lemons, make lemonade

There is no doubt that the loss of a close relationship is an enormously impactful life event that elicits emotional suffering. It is well-recognised that this type of loss significantly impacts a person's emotional well-being, causing psychological distress and decreasing their satisfaction with life.[2] We know that the loss of a relationship is among the highest-rating stressful events that we can encounter as humans.[3] When we suffer, as you have, it is only natural that you would want to find meaning in that suffering. In an ideal world, you can learn from it so that this painful life experience can be a source of personal growth. The idea that good can come from hardship is age-old, and I think represents the remarkable human capacity to adapt, respond, and thrive. That doesn't mean that it is *easy*, but the most important lessons never are unfortunately. However, humans facing difficult situations are capable of positive change, of not just surviving a difficult experience and returning to normal functioning, but of growing *beyond* their normal functioning. This is the concept of post-traumatic growth.[4]

This is what I want for you. You have put so much effort into understanding your own attachment origins and how your last relationship might have become tangled up in a negative cycle that stole your connection. You have laboured over the processing of your feelings about this loss, working through anger and sadness to fully accept the reality of your situation. Now it is time to grow beyond your starting point, for all this hardship to launch you onto a new path. A path that feels right for you, where your past can help you and your future pulls and urges you forward bravely and securely. Learning and hope do go hand in hand.

We don't grow if the lesson doesn't fully grab our attention. Your pain is taking you somewhere important. In fact, an essential element that determines if a person experiences growth from a trauma, is how disorganising it is to their inner world. When something goes wrong in your life, so wrong that it challenges all your assumptions about the world, about right and wrong, good and bad, about the order of things, about your place in the world, then it is powerful enough to change your view of everything. I can only assume that your loss has all those ingredients (or you wouldn't be reaching for this book). When the traumatic event you face exceeds your ability to manage, then it truly becomes fertile ground for growth. As awful as it is, the kind of suffering that shatters your core assumptions is more likely to lead to growth than other less painful life lessons. This is a fundamental part of our human make-up. Where there is pain of this nature, there is the opportunity for this to transform into a resource for growth and meaning. This is more than just putting up with a bad situation, gritting your teeth and resisting being knocked down. We are talking about transcending the present circumstance and making a deeply profound improvement as a direct result of this adversity. We are talking about transformation. It's risky this stuff, as it challenges and exposes us mightily, right down to our core. Who wouldn't feel vulnerable?

It is not enough to have just faced hardship. Transformation happens as result of *how* a person faces that hardship. This is in no way a judgement of you, it is a statement of fact about growth. It is the struggle with the reality of the trauma and how you confront and adapt to the changes required of you that determines how much you will grow from it. Growing from a trauma doesn't take away the pain caused by it or mean that you have to be grateful for what has happened (far from it), but that the two states of pain and growth can and do co-exist. I am not suggesting you ever need to feel gratitude that this has happened, but I am hoping that all this pain and difficulty can be put to good use. We put the pain to good use by being willing to examine the shattered expectations and assumptions, by being willing to feel the big feelings, and by taking action that helps you to adjust your life. This means accepting the loss and stepping out of destructive patterns that keep you stuck in either experiencing your emotions "too much" or "not enough" (as we looked at in Chapters 4 and 5). This means reconciling and altering your belief system and redirecting your attachment needs – shuffling your inner world to accommodate this new reality. This is enormously tough work, and you are well on your way. If you've made it this far in the book with me, then you deserve a huge "well done!" Now just a bit further to go.

When people attempt to do this work, then they can find meaning in the most harrowing of experiences. Some of the benefits of post-traumatic growth are an increased appreciation of life, a realigning of priorities, closer and more meaningful relationships with others, increased empathy and compassion for others, increased awareness of your own personal strength, tuning into your spirituality, and forging a new direction in life.

Now that is awe-inspiring adaptation in action! These positive changes reflect an ongoing life-long process of the development of wisdom. They represent a happy by-product of adversity; not merely surviving but flourishing. If that sounds too good to be true, remember the self-exploration and pain you have experienced (or are now experiencing), and it will become clear that these positives are very hard-earned.

Reflection 1

To help with this process, I would like to invite you to reflect on what you have discovered so far as you have worked your way through the previous chapters.

- *Which of your attachment needs were unmet in past relationships?*
- *How did you signal your needs, and did you do this in way that fed into a negative pattern with your ex-partners?*
- *What have you come to learn about your own attachment strategies?*
- *What have you discovered about your deepest needs, longings, and fears as you have connected with your angry protest and despair?*
- *Have you come to learn that you need to <u>tune into your painful feelings more</u> or to gain <u>more working distance from</u> them in order to best process the emotional and practical elements of your grief?*

Making meaning for growth

How you engage with your inner world in the processing of a negative event determines whether you become stuck and dwell on the negative aspects in a ruminative way, or whether you process and move through the pain to a place of reorganisation. The severity of your emotional distress following the loss of this relationship does not impair your ability to grow from it. As an example, more than half of the female partners in a study who had experienced betrayal of an agreement of sexual exclusivity by their male partners met DSM-V diagnostic criteria for post-traumatic stress disorder. The more severely they rated their hurt and the more disruptive it was to their beliefs and expectations, the more they displayed post-traumatic growth.[5] In other words, you can be really distressed and experience growth at the same time. What the researchers identified as a valuable contributor to the process of growth was a person's capacity to let go of old unhelpful ways of evaluating what happened such as, "It was all my fault" or "This happened because I am a bad person," and being able to find new meaning in it such as, "We both contributed to the relationship distress" or "I was not being my best self and I am learning from this experience."

These ideas synergise with our discoveries in Chapter 5 when looking at the grieving process and how much emotional processing is helpful and when it can become a hindrance. The way we engage with our painful feelings and the meaning we make from our experiences are so important in whether we remain stuck in old self-defeating patterns or whether we can break out of them and forge new patterns moving forward. Finding a way to honour your emotional experience and not become swallowed up by unhelpful themes seems to be a delicate balance. It is clear from the research that what has been termed "ruminative coping" is related to heightened distress and delayed recovery from negative life events.[6] This kind of thinking involves chewing over what is not available to you now that this bad thing has happened, on what has been lost, laying blame, and seeking answers to (usually) impossible questions. It involves literally "marinating" in the hopelessness of the situation and on what could have been or should have been. This is a black hole of despair that creates its own weather patterns and it's always overcast. Now please don't go judging yourself for doing this, as it is part of the grieving process. But importantly, you don't want to get stuck there indefinitely. There is a difference between wallowing and immersing. Wallowing is a *helpless* process that has the risk of being pulled under, whereas immersing is a *conscious act of being with* your experience to learn from it and grow. **Immersing is intentional and deliberate, while wallowing is not.**

If you immerse yourself in your natural distress in order to reflect and learn, then this can lead to learning powerful lessons. When you can focus on your humanity and shortcomings to not deepen your despair and self-recrimination, but to mobilise yourself to learn and to make changes, then that same rumination has a very different outcome. In this way, our distress can force us to hold a mirror up and to see ourselves differently in the reflection. This shattering of our illusions about ourselves can either send us spiralling into a pit of shame or can move us into self-growth. It is a brave undertaking that admittedly requires some grit, but if you do this in the spirit of growth and with a dose of self-compassion (we *all* make mistakes and we *all* behave in ways we are not proud of), then it can be truly life changing. A study found that reflection in this way was associated with increased personal growth after a breakup and an increased ability to detach from the ex-partner and to be open to new relationships. The researchers concluded that self-reflection may motivate a course of self-improvement that includes ownership of one's own role in the ending of the relationship and the development of relationship-maintenance skills by carefully attending to past relationship mistakes.[7] This is the stuff of the "dark night of the soul" that can be excruciating *and* powerfully transformative. We will never get there by being harsh and cruel towards ourselves – we only achieve this with compassion and self-care. We are going to look at that idea more in Chapter 7.

Reflection 2

Now that you are thinking more about how you might interact with your inner world, ask yourself:

- *What am I learning about myself and my role in this breakup?*
- *How does it feel to acknowledge my shortcomings?*
- *Do I tend to fall into a pit of shame, or can I keep my balance to look into the mirror and learn from this?*
- *What do I need to work on for my own growth and to take into my next relationship?*

Forgiveness and letting go

An important part of the reorganisation of your inner world and detachment from a close relationship is making sense of the loss and achieving distance from the intensity of the emotional fall-out. This is especially difficult if you have been wronged by your ex-partner and have not felt heard, or if your hurt has not been acknowledged. When someone we loved and trusted hurts us or rejects us, we tend to feel pain, hostility, and anger, which can all translate into thoughts of revenge. We can become caught in destructive patterns of avoidance or aggressive pursuit in an attempt for some relief from this hurt. When this anger is directed at ourselves, then this is especially difficult to resolve. While this is a *protective* coping strategy designed to keep us safe, it can lead us into unproductive behaviours that keep us dwelling on hurts that cannot be resolved, and this can actually reinforce our distress. Forgiveness, as part of your recovery from loss and hurt, can be an important part of the process.

Forgiveness is an intentional strategy that interrupts patterns of avoidance and revenge, decreases negative thoughts and behaviours towards someone who has wronged you, and promotes relationship cohesion.[8] Forgiveness does not mean condoning or excusing bad behaviour or minimising the devastating impact of another's actions. Forgiving someone is a transformative process that involves a deliberate and intentional attempt to understand the hurtful event, to take into account the other person's perspective, and to understand the context in which they were hurtful. This means making a concerted effort to understand and empathise with the other and to alter any negative opinions you might be holding about their behaviour towards you.[9] This can be a challenging process, but the benefits of forgiveness can be profound. Forgiveness is associated with a host of positive physical and mental health outcomes such as reduced stress, lower resting heart rate, and greater life satisfaction, as well as having a positive impact on relationship functioning.[10] For separated partners who are co-parenting children, forgiveness has been found to be an important ingredient in being able to form a productive co-parenting relationship with lower levels of conflict that allows children to better adapt to the separation.[11] After a divorce, forgiveness has been related to lower levels of anger and depression, more positive post-divorce communication, and higher levels of well-being.[12] Clearly, this is a preferable situation to be in as you renegotiate your relationship with your ex-partner and make sense of this loss.

How easily you can achieve forgiveness depends on many factors related to the relationship, the nature of the hurt, your experiences with previous hurts, and much more. However, your *attachment strategies* can also play a role. Research has shown us that those with secure attachment strategies find it easier to forgive transgressions because they tend to hold more positive views of others and to interpret their behaviour more benignly. They are also more likely to use effective emotional regulation strategies and to turn to others for support in times of distress. As I have mentioned before, if you are lucky enough to have been raised with secure attachment figures who helped you to learn secure attachment strategies, then they deserve a huge hug now, as not all are this lucky.

People with anxious attachment strategies tend to struggle more with forgiveness. This is partly because, as we know, they are likely to feel higher levels of distress and to be more engulfed in their emotional experience, but it is also because they are more likely to dwell on these hurts and to attribute negative meaning to the other's actions. This leaves very little room for processing this hurt in a new light. In addition to this, people with anxious attachment strategies are likely to keep reaching out to their ex-partner for resolution, which only heightens their distress and isolation. Alternatively, for people with avoidant attachment strategies, forgiveness is at odds with their usual tendency of dismissing or suppressing their vulnerable emotions. While they are less likely to dwell on hurtful events than those with anxious attachment strategies, their lack of emotional engagement might inhibit them from being able to find the much-needed empathy for the other's perspective in order for forgiveness to take place.

Empathy for the other's experience seems to be very important in achieving a sense of forgiveness. Being able to understand the other person's experience and modify previously held assumptions about their motives or their personality makes forgiving more likely. When we empathise with a partner who has hurt us, our desire for retribution often evaporates; if not entirely, it is substantially reduced. Seeing their humanity and acknowledging that good people can make grave mistakes takes the wind right out of our righteously indignant sails. So, in this way, forgiveness relies on being able to take the other's perspective and to form an alternative explanation for the hurtful person's intent and actions. It has been shown that those with a greater ability to empathise with their partner were more likely to forgive, and those who struggled to let go of negative interpretations about their partner's intentions were less likely to forgive. That said, it is really difficult to empathise with another person when we are in our reactive, protective state. This is why forgiveness might rely on some working distance from the heat of the emotions and might require the passage of time and the cool light of day. After all, how you interact with your emotional world will determine whether you wallow in blame and negative attributions about the other's intentions or whether you can immerse yourself in their point of view and find a more neutral way of seeing their actions (along with and in spite of your own pain).

It is important to note that *you* deserve the same consideration. My role as your guide at this moment is to reinforce this.
The aim of all this is not to tell you to act like Mother Theresa! I
urge you to look at your own actions in your past relationship
through the same kind and benign lens so that you might be able
to give yourself the gift of empathy and understanding inherent
in any forgiveness. I have not met a single person who is not har-
bouring some shameful or guilty feelings about their actions in
their relationships. None of us are at our best when we are in a
reactive state and feeling that our most important relationship is
threatened. Even though it is excruciating, when we can reflect
on the parts of our experience that are hardest to be with, our
own guilt and shame, we can learn and grow. Feelings of guilt
stem from knowing that you have hurt another person you care
about. Guilty feelings are useful signals because they alert us that
we have caused another harm and need to make amends to right
a wrong. Even if we are not making amends in order to
strengthen an ongoing attachment bond, repair work when we
have caused harm to an ex-partner will be enormously helpful in
allowing each of you to move forwards in a new way without old
hurts tainting your redefined relationship. On the other hand,
feelings of shame, while having the capacity to send us spiralling
into self-loathing, are important signals that we have stepped
away from our own principles. Shame is a message to us that we
need to reflect on whether we have done something we are not
proud of. Shame is all about holding yourself to account and
acknowledging that you are not happy with who you are right
now. Rather than motivating us to make amends with another,
shame motivates us to retreat and to self-reflect. This process can
become destructive when it involves hiding our true self and
turning away from others, but it can become transformative
when it propels us to improve, to settle things with ourselves, and
to carry ourselves differently in the world.

As you can see, forgiveness, far from excusing hurtful
behaviour, can be extremely helpful in processing and moving on
from a relationship. It can help you to move forwards in new
ways. Being able to see hurtful acts in a new light forms part of
the "work" of processing this negative event in a way that will
lead to trauma growth rather than stuckness. Having an
expanded view of hurtful acts and developing empathy and
understanding for yourself and your ex-partner will set you free
from negative patterns. This will give you the best chance of

being able to maintain a relationship with your ex-partner if you so choose or if life circumstances require that of you. Forgiveness will encourage you to grow as a person and transcend the hardship you have faced, stronger and wiser for it. In other words, forgiveness is both positive for others and yourself. But, be fair on yourself, forgiveness is a "work in progress" for some time for most of us. We are all human after all.

Reflection 3

Think about hurts that have been inflicted on you in close relationships:

- *What have you come to understand about why the other might have acted so hurtfully?*
- *Without condoning hurtful acts, have you been able to feel into the other's experience to gain some more perspective and empathy for them?*
- *Do you think that you can forgive them in order to set yourself free from this relationship?*
- *Are you able to give the same care and consideration to yourself?*
- *What have you come to learn about yourself through this process of forgiveness?*

Reorganisation and detachment

Part of the work to reorganise the inner structures, tendencies, and expectations you hold is to shift your natural need to reach out to your ex-partner as a source of co-regulation in times of need. To break the pattern of turning to your ex-partner for your felt sense of security can be difficult, but break it you must, in order for you to fully detach. A crucial task of successful detachment is managing your own emotional dysregulation in new ways.[13] Now that your partner is no longer a coping resource, you have to actively work on self-regulating, which means calming your emotional storms on your own a little more than you might have done before, as well as building attachment bonds with safe others. This requires you to redefine the other person in your mind as no longer part of your "inner circle" of special attachment figures. They are no longer able to be accessible to you, responsive to your needs, or engaged with you on an emotional level. They cannot be your safe haven or secure base. While they might remain in your life in some way, your bond needs to be "undone" and renegotiated so as to release you both from your close emotional tie. No longer are your hearts and nervous systems entwined – your reach and impact are now lessoned.

To prevent further hurt and misunderstandings, it is likely becoming clear that it is essential that you accept this reality and redirect your attachment efforts towards others who can be accessible, emotionally responsive, and engaged with you. This is the very undoing of the attachment bond that we have mentioned. Reorganisation requires you to find a way to soothe yourself that does not impede your forward movement with the tasks of life and of establishing new connections. What that looks like exactly, is as individual as each person reading this book. No matter how it looks, reorganising your view of the other to fit with the new reality of your relationship and redirecting your attachment needs is the final task in the work of grief and loss.

In Chapter 1, we highlighted that as a human, you have an inbuilt need to connect with safe others and it is painful to lose a connection with someone special. Improving your ability to self-soothe, to regulate your inner emotional world, and to tune into the wisdom embedded in your experience is part of being able to process and reorganise how you interact with vulnerable emotions because it utilises yourself as a coping resource. While that is an important skill that we all need to learn, building secure attachments with other humans is vital to our ability to cope with adversity because this provides the most efficient way of regulating emotions. We need to be able to soothe ourselves *and* turn to others for our attachment needs. One feeds the other, the more we know that we have people to turn to, the less we need them and the more we can be there for ourselves. Similarly, the more we can be there for ourselves, the more we feel okay about turning to others and letting them help us when we need it. We know that having others to take our vulnerable emotions to is essential for growing beyond a negative life event. Research has shown that being able to share the most painful and frightening experiences with safe others increases the likelihood of post-traumatic growth.[14] This process is thought to help with the cognitive processing of a negative life event. In other words, having a supportive sounding board in a trusted other is a huge advantage in processing big feelings. It not only helps you to make sense of this event and to reorganise your inner world to adjust to this loss, but it might even help you to grow stronger for it.

While forming attachment bonds with other people is helpful and needed, I think it is important to spend time on the work of grief and not to rush into another romantic relationship too soon after a loss of this magnitude. We know that those of us with anxious attachment strategies are likely to find the process of detaching from a partner more difficult than those with avoidant attachment strategies. There is some evidence that people with anxious attachment strategies are more likely to search early on for a replacement attachment figure as a way of managing the anxiety inherent in being without a romantic partner.[15] Given that replacing a lost love with another could seem to be the answer to feelings of loneliness and isolation, this could be a temptation for some people. While this may ameliorate the pain and hurt, it could be doing you a disservice by also reducing the drive to find meaning from this important life event. Remember, where there is suffering, there is real opportunity for growth and future happiness. In a way, intentionally building a wider range of attachment figures rather than one romantic connection that meets all your attachment needs might provide opportunity for more self-growth as well as providing insurance against relying on only one person to be your "everything." The process of healing fully before embarking on a new close relationship allows for you to be intentional in the way you seek out and carry yourself in your next relationship. This might prevent repetitive patterns and stand you in good stead for creating the relationship you have been longing for. Don't do it until you read Chapters 7 and 8 at least!

Reflection 4

- *Can you tell the story of the loss of this relationship in a way that honours both of you (without condoning unacceptable behaviours)?*
- *What are you learning about yourself and your needs through this process?*
- *Do you notice yourself wanting to turn to your ex-partner for emotional support?*
- *How could you redirect those attachment needs?*
- *How could you redefine your view of your ex-partner now?*

- *Who could you take your attachment needs to now?*
- *What do you need from yourself to help you to be a safe place for yourself right now?*

Your survival narrative

As you process the loss you have faced and spend time reflecting on hurts in ways that allow for forgiveness of yourself and of your ex-partner, you are undertaking the amazing work of reorganising your inner world. You are accepting the reality of this loss and reconciling the negative elements of the experience. You are beginning to redefine the relationship and to learn and grow from the lessons learned in it. You are creating a new narrative of this loss and of yourself within this experience that leads to growth. Instead of seeing the loss as evidence of failure and yourself as potentially unlovable, my hope is that you are now able to see your past relationship with new eyes, that you are able to embrace your partner's and your own humanity and to construct a new narrative of how it went wrong. Hopefully, you will see how you lost your way, how your bond might have been damaged, and how you have survived the loss, and are learning and growing as a result. This hopeful narrative is empowering and restorative. It is imbued with compassion for yourself as an attachment being, a perfectly imperfect human with valid needs. It carries with it lessons from the past and looks to the future with optimism and wisdom. This is amazing, brutal, gut-wrenching, and invigorating work, and I am confident that it will lead you to grow out of this adversity.

In achieving this important milestone in the recovery process, you are reorganising your inner world and redirecting your attachment energies. You have grieved for this loss, and your pain has honoured the love you brought to this bond. Your suffering is evidence of your remarkable capacity for love and for growth. Now you are opening up to new opportunities; opportunities for knowing yourself more deeply and for showing up in your next close relationship in a completely new way. This is rubber-meets-the-road change in action. It is my sincerest hope that you are now finding a way to make sense of this loss that honours the story of your time together and the contribution you made to that bond. I hope that you are being gentler with yourself, and that you are finding a way to use this loss for growth.

The principle of thriving out of adversity is your survival narrative. This is a coherent summary infused with humility, compassion, empathy, and validation, which describes your learnings from this harrowing life event and allows you to let go and shift your focus from your rear-vision mirror to the road ahead. Take some time to reflect on how far you have come since Chapter 1. Be sure to acknowledge your willingness to immerse yourself in this process; not all are so willing. Your growth is a testament to your hard work.

- *What is your survival narrative?*
  I hope your survival narrative has these elements... "I love deeply, and I hurt deeply, and I am strong enough to cope, and I am not beaten. Good things are coming for me, and not only do I deserve them, I welcome them with open arms and an open heart." This is not a mantra, it is a summary of where you are now after a good deal of difficult and often painful work.

Chapter 6 takeaways

- We know that relationship loss is among the highest-rating stressful events that we can encounter as humans.
- Post-traumatic growth is the concept that humans facing difficult situations are capable of positive change, of not just surviving a difficult experience and returning to normal functioning, but of growing beyond their normal functioning.
- It is not enough to have just faced hardship; transformation happens as result of how a person faces that hardship. It is the struggle with the reality of the trauma and how you confront and adapt to the changes required of you that determines how much you will grow from it.
- The way we engage with our painful feelings and the meaning we make from our experiences determine whether we remain stuck in old self-defeating patterns or whether we can break out of them and forge new patterns moving forward.
- Forgiveness is an intentional strategy that interrupts patterns of avoidance and vengeance, decreases negative thoughts and behaviours towards someone who has wronged you, and promotes detachment. If you remain in contact with your ex-partner, forgiveness promotes ongoing relationship cohesion.

- Forgiving someone can be a transformative process that involves a deliberate and intentional attempt to understand the hurtful event, taking into account the other person's perspective and the context in which they were hurtful.
- Forgiveness of yourself or another involves a willingness to see the hurtful acts in a new way, with empathy for the inherent struggle, and with more benign attributions. It does not mean excusing abhorrent behaviour.
- Reorganising your view of your ex-partner is an important part of redirecting your attachment needs away from your lost love and towards other attachment figures.
- Your revised view of your struggle, your learnings, and your growth is your survival narrative. This is a powerful symbol of your post-traumatic growth, and it will ensure that your future benefits from your past.

Notes

1. Bowlby, J. (1979). *The making and breaking of affectional bonds.* London: Tavistock.
2. Rhoades, G. K., Dush, C. M. K., Atkins, D. C., Stanley, S. M., & Markman, H. J. (2011). Breaking up is hard to do: The impact of unmarried relationship dissolution on mental health and life satisfaction. *Journal of Family Psychology, 25*(3), 366–374.
3. Dyrdal, G. M., Røysamb, E., Nes, R. B., & Vittersø, J. (2019). When life happens: Investigating short and long-term effects of life stressors on life satisfaction in a large sample of Norwegian mothers. *Journal of Happiness Studies, 20,* 1689–1715.
4. Tedeschi, R. G, & Calhoun, L. G. (2004). Posttraumatic growth: Conceptual foundations and empirical evidence. *Psychological Inquiry, 15*(1), 1–18.
5. Laaser, D., Putney, H. L., Bundick, M., Delmonico, D. L., & Griffin, E. J. (2017). Posttraumatic growth in relationally betrayed women. *Journal of Marital and Family Therapy, 43*(3), 435–447.
6. Nolen-Hoeksema, S., Parker, L. E., & Larson, J. (1994). Ruminative coping with depressed mood following loss. *Journal of Personality and Social Psychology, 67*(1), 92–104.
7. Marshall, T. C., Bejanyan, K., & Ferenczi, N. (2013). Attachment styles and personal growth following romantic breakups: The mediating roles of distress, rumination, and tendency to rebound. *PLOS ONE, 8*(9), e75161.
8. Guzmán-González, M., Wlodarczyk, A., Contreras, P., Rivera-Ottenberger, D., & Garrido, L. (2019). Romantic attachment and

adjustment to separation: The role of forgiveness of the former partner. *Journal of Child and Family Studies, 28*(1), 3011–3021.

9. Kimmes, J. G., & Durtschi, J. A. (2016). Forgiveness in romantic relationships: The roles of attachment, empathy and attributions. *Journal of Marital and Family Therapy, 42*(4), 645–658.

10. Hirst, S. L., Hepper, E. G., & Tenenbaum, H. R. (2019). Attachment dimensions and forgiveness of others: A meta-analysis. *Journal of Social & Personal Relationships, 36*(11–12), 0265407519841716. DOI: 10.1177/0265407519841716

11. Visser, M., Finkenauer, C., Schoemaker, K., Kluwer, E., van der Rijken, R., van Lawick, J., Bom, H., de Schipper, J. C., & Lamers-Winkelman, F. (2017). I'll never forgive you: High conflict divorce, social network, and co-parenting conflicts. *Journal of Child and Family Studies, 26*(11), 3055–3066.

12. Yárnoz-Yaben, S., Garmendia, A., & Comino, P. (2016). Looking at the bright side: Forgiveness and subjective well-being in divorced Spanish parents. *Journal of Happiness Studies, 17*(5), 1905–1919.

13. Sbarra, D. A., & Hazan, C. (2008). Coregulation, dysregulation, self-regulation: An integrative analysis and empirical agenda for understanding adult attachment, separation, loss, and recovery. *Personality and Social Psychology Review, 12*(2), 141–167.

14. Tedeschi, R. G., & Calhoun, L. G. (2004). Posttraumatic growth: Conceptual foundations and empirical evidence. *Psychological Inquiry, 15*(1), 1–18.

15. Davis, D., Shaver, P. R., & Vernon, M. L. (2003). Physical, emotional and behavioural reactions to breaking up: The roles of gender, age, emotional involvement, and attachment style. *Personality & Social Psychology Bulletin, 29*(7), 871–884.

SEVEN

Earning security with yourself

So far, we have explored how to work through and to process the very personal emotional fallout of the loss of someone special to you. You have toiled through the painful emotions involved and have learned to understand your reactions and your emotions by looking at them through an attachment lens. I imagine this has been very difficult and challenging. But remember, you have done so well to examine this. I applaud your tenacity and your courage in being willing to do the hard yards to heal and to learn from this loss. Our key aim has been to help you to healthily process this loss so that you can learn about yourself and grow from this hardship. We have learned that in order to adjust to the loss of an attachment figure, it is important to be able to pay attention to your inner emotional world as well as attending to the practical aspects of life. We now know that *reorganising* your internal world in such a way that your lost love is no longer the person you take your attachment needs to is essential for successful detachment and moving on. But above all, it is becoming clearer and clearer that successful adaptation to this loss involves being with your emotions in a way that is neither *overwhelming* nor *dismissive*. We can see that being engulfed by or (the opposite) ignoring your painful feelings can be a barrier to recovery from loss and might inhibit your opportunity for learning and growth.

Getting the balance right where you can tune into your emotional world productively is easier if you are lucky enough to have secure attachment strategies; however, it can be trickier if no one helped you to learn this balance through your earliest attachment bonds. In this chapter, we are going to look at how to navigate your emotional world in a balanced way. It's time to hang out with yourself, to befriend your inner world, and to become a source of support and security for yourself. I am going

DOI: 10.4324/9781003264163-11

to help you to continue to get to know yourself better and to explore who you are *without* this relationship. Together, we will tune into the beauty of your inner emotional world and hold the painful places with compassion. We will do this in order to mine the wisdom and strength to be found there. We will look at using all this wonderful attunement with yourself to guide you to your needs and values, so that they can direct your path forward in new ways.

What is the point of emotion anyway?

Sometimes, emotions can lead us to do the strangest things. Grown adults can throw tantrums worthy of any self-respecting two-year-old over the lack of salt and vinegar chips in the cupboard because, "You knew they were for me!" Emotions can make us do many, often baffling things such as hurling ourselves out of perfectly good aeroplanes for a sense of exhilaration, yelling at someone in the supermarket for taking the last packet of toilet paper in a pandemic, or brawls in quiet neighbourhoods over the positioning of a fence. Sayings like "in the heat of the moment" indicate how common it is for people to become swept up in their emotions and do things they (we) later regret. Emotions can frighten us with their seeming irrationality and their ability to make us "take leave of our senses." In many cultures, emotions are considered a reasonable driver of behaviour (for example, justifiable homicide as a "crime of passion" in France). In others, certain emotions are considered undesirable. Partly because of this, some people have developed a derisive attitude to emotions and have prized rationality over tuning into our emotional world. From early in life, we receive the message that emotions need to be curbed and not given free rein. We learn and absorb the idea that emotions get in the way of adaptive functioning and need to be managed to prevent them from having a negative influence on our lives. This could not be further from the truth. Also, this does not contend with gender-based biases that are beyond the scope of this book.

Far from being irrational and inconsequential to humans, emotions are vital to our survival. Emotions perform several crucial functions that enhance our well-being and maintain our social connections. Firstly, emotions are an adaptive resource because they keep us informed about our well-being based on feedback from our internal and external worlds, like a sentinel keeping watch over us. Our emotions are part of a complex messaging system that provides us with feedback about our environment (our external world) and about our internal needs and goals.[1] Emotions let us know if we are safe and let us know when something doesn't feel right for us. Think about the concept of "gut feeling" or intuition – this is an emotional signal that is not part of a "rational" thought, it is a *feeling* about something that usually compels us to act protectively. The same intuition that tells us not to walk down that particular dark alley also tells us that a particular decision isn't right for us. Emotions signal to us about our safety and our needs, and without them we would be in trouble. Sue Johnson, the founder of Emotionally Focused Therapy, says that "being *tuned out* of emotional experience is like navigating through life without a compass.[2]"

Secondly, emotions perform a vital role in helping us to know about our needs in the first place. Bowlby asserted that the main function of emotion was to communicate our needs, motives, and priorities – *to ourselves and to others*.[3] Our emotions grab hold of our attention and alert us that something isn't right in our inner or outer world. This signal prompts us to pay attention and make meaning about our experience. They focus us on what is relevant to our needs and wants, engaging our attention in an absorbing way. Emotions have a way of commanding our attention. For instance, you can be fully immersed in your most favourite book, but if you suddenly see a huge spider on the wall beside you, you will be completely unable to concentrate on the book. Your emotional system is fired up and alarm bells are clamouring for you to move away from this threat. You will be moving before your conscious mind has even fully registered a threat. Not only ensuring our safety, our emotions help us to know what we want and need by helping us to make decisions. Many believe that decision-making and problem-solving is a purely rational process, but in fact, it is underpinned by emotion. When presented with several viable options, often it is how we *feel* that determines the course of action that best fits for us.

Thirdly, emotions allow us to signal efficiently to other humans, and so play an important role in social communication between humans. Right from birth, emotions are a primary signalling system from baby to caregiver about their needs, and from caregiver to baby about their intentions, safety, and love. In this way, our emotions connect us together and our emotional regulation becomes entwined. Soothing one soothes the other. Our nervous systems are built to be sensitive to emotional non-verbal cues from others, especially vocal tone and facial expression. We are wired to find contact with a safe "other" to be regulating and calming to the in-built alarm system of our autonomic nervous system.[4] Our social connections rely on emotional signals to communicate, commune, and soothe. Emotion brings connection to life by regulating self and other and adds colour to experiences that arguably give life much of its meaning.[5]

Finally, emotions, both good and bad, comfortable or uncomfortable, push us to move in certain directions or to take certain actions. The word emotion literally means "to move." Emotion energises us to take action in the service of our needs. When we are experiencing positive emotions, like joy, love, excitement, or curiosity, then we are typically feeling good. When we are experiencing negative emotions such as sadness, hurt, anger, loneliness, or fear, then we are typically feeing bad. How we feel influences what we do, which in turn influences those around us. Fear tends to prime us to run or to freeze, anger will motivate us to approach or to stand our ground, sadness will prompt us to seek comfort or to retreat to soothe ourselves, shame will promote hiding, joy will encourage relaxed engagement and openness, and surprise will evoke curiosity. Emotions are the spark that sets off a chain reaction of meaning-making and action.

As you can see, emotions are important to our well-being as humans. Being able to engage with our own internal world rather than ignoring or denying parts of it is key in finding the meaning in our experience. However, this doesn't mean that we have to be in our emotional world at all times; this would not be practical at all! Therefore, being able to manage and regulate our emotions is an important skill for living. This involves being able to listen to our emotional signals *and* it means being able to temporarily shelve them when needed. Although emotions are very important to humans, we can't always give them the attention they deserve at any given time or simply let them run rife, especially if this meant interference with other important tasks of life. Being able to return to our emotional signals to process them when able is part of the process of emotional regulation.[6]

As I see it, there are two key components to successful emotional regulation. The first is being able to *self*-regulate (soothe yourself) and the second is being able to *co*-regulate with a safe other. We learn how to approach both of these important tasks in our earliest attachment relationships, and this ability continues to develop in every meaningful relationship we have throughout our life. Being able to self-soothe means being able to turn up the heat on our emotions by paying attention to them or turning down the heat if they are so loud that we cannot access the meaning in our emotional experiences. Let's start by looking at what your earliest relationships taught you about managing and interacting with your emotions.

How your attachment strategies shape your relationship with your emotions

Managing intense, hard-to-hold emotions is a universal human struggle. It is the stuff of poetry, songs, and folklore. Going on a quest to find inner wisdom and letting that set the course for a meaningful life is a key theme of popular stories held up as examples of successful living. This shows us how important these ideas are to us, and we know how elusive success in these areas of human experience can be. Being able to wrangle our feelings and challenge ourselves to live our best life is something that we often aspire to and can all grapple with. The trickiest part of navigating emotions is being *with* our uncomfortable inner experiences. Staying there, and holding our toes to the fire of our most intense emotional experiences, is not for the faint of heart. However, this is what is often required to find the meaning in the experience. The most efficient way to learn how to do this is to be shown by a safe other early in life. For the rest of us, we have to develop this skill ourselves and often with the help of special others throughout our life.

As we know, our experience of turning to our attachment figures throughout life teaches us how to manage our emotions, whether reaching out for help from another is a good idea, and about our self-worth. When someone can be with us in our most unsettling emotional moments, we learn that we can ride out the storm of our inner world, that our pain matters, that it does pass, and that there is a beautiful logic in our emotional experience if we can stay with it. Right from infancy, if we are soothed by a caring "stronger, wiser other," then we internalise their soothing ability and become more adept at riding the wave of our own emotions and regulating ourselves (and also others). Being soothed by a responsive caregiver allows a child to, in effect, "borrow" their caregiver's prefrontal cortex. As the caregiver soothes the child and calmly navigates the emotional turmoil, this calms the child's nervous system, and it impacts their brain by "showing the way," which sets up the neural systems involved in regulating emotion.[7] In this way, the caregiver demonstrates secure attachment strategies, and the child absorbs them.

As adults, people with *secure* attachment strategies are likely to have experienced their early caregivers as responsive and engaged, and will have internalised a sense of their own value and worthiness of love and support. Due to being shown how to be with their emotional world, they are less likely to fear their emotional storms because they have a sense that they can handle them. They also know that, if it gets too rocky, they have others to turn to for assistance. Because they tend to have confidence in their ability to manage their emotions, people with secure attachment strategies don't need to rely on others for approval or assistance unless they really need them. When vulnerable or uncertain, because their attachment figures have been compassionate towards them, they can treat themselves and others with the same consideration. As a result, they are less negatively impacted by mistakes or criticism or setbacks because their sense of self-worth is relatively stable, and they can offer themselves soothing and reassurance. This internal composure and self-assurance means that they can be with their emotional experience and feel it fully, no matter whether it is good, bad, or otherwise. They become proficient at *tuning into* their emotions when needed, and gaining *working distance* from them when needed. This is the art of emotional regulation. We are going to build your capacity to do this.

Research shows us that people with *avoidant* attachment strategies are likely to manage their emotions by holding them at bay, trying to keep their vulnerable feelings distant or suppressed. They have learned that they have to cope alone with their struggles, so it is best not to "poke the bear" of their inner world. They see emotions as best suppressed rather than engaged with flexibly to enhance well-being. To do this, they have to avoid anything that could bring alive painful or hard to handle emotions like fear, sadness, shame, uncertainty, or self-doubt. However, we now know that we can't selectively suppress emotions, so people with avoidant attachment strategies can end up suppressing *all* emotions, even the *positive* ones. As a consequence, they do not get to savour wonderful experiences or to find the meaning in tough experiences. They have learned that they must remain steadfast in their self-reliance and keep a distance from others, especially those who matter because they could "wake the bear" of their emotional world. This means that people with avoidant attachment strategies have learned over their life to not tune into their emotional world, and to not reach out to others for support. As a result, they do not benefit from paying attention to their emotional experiences or by finding the meaning in them. They miss out on crucial information about their deepest needs, and might choose their path of action based on general ideas about what a person "should" do, rather than what is truly aligned with their *own* needs and goals.

For example, Bill is struggling with a loss of meaning in his life since retiring from his job of 30 years. He suspects that the loss of his vocation is triggering feelings of sadness, loss, and failure but he has learned to steer clear of such painful emotions. So, he busies himself with hobbies in the hope that they will distract him and give him a new sense of purpose. Without tuning into his inner world to connect with the true origin of the pain for him, his activities never quite soothe the pain and feel empty and pointless. Even if they were enjoyable, he is not able to fully connect with this experience either. This then perpetuates his lost feelings, and he develops a sense of hopelessness as well. Without paying attention to his emotional signals, he cannot savour good moments or get to the bottom of what is missing for him. Therefore, he cannot fully process the meaning in his emotional signals or learn from them. He can't give himself what he is most needing at a heart level because he is not tuned-in to this part of himself. As a result, any attempt to manage his emotions is hollow for him, and only serves to perpetuate his stuckness.

Research also shows us that people with *anxious* attachment strategies tend to have little belief in their own ability to manage their emotional world without the help of another. They are used to having to amplify their signals to get on the other's radar, which can leave them overwhelmed by the intensity of their own emotional world. Their heightened levels of distress can interrupt the process of making sense of emotional experiences and extracting the meaning from them. In fact, people with anxious attachment strategies have been shown to have difficulty with identifying and describing their feelings because their inner world can feel chaotic, and it can be hard to differentiate between intense emotions. This can leave them feeling very vulnerable to threatening events, and pessimistic about their own ability to cope. As a result, those who use anxious attachment strategies might not develop a confidence in their own ability to manage their emotions. It is very demoralising to be consumed with painful emotion, and to not believe that you can find any wisdom in it by yourself. This blocks a person with anxious attachment strategies from finding the adaptive possibilities in their emotional reactions.

For instance, Prue longs to make brave changes to her life by stepping out of safe "ruts" and going on an adventure of travelling overseas. When she even lets herself *think* about the possibility of taking such a big step, she becomes immobilised by fear as her worst imaginings of becoming lost in a foreign country without any money, and being at the mercy of predators, swamp her. Her fear becomes more acute as she becomes hyper-focused on these terrible outcomes, and how devastating they would be. She becomes so uncomfortable with the level of distress that she cannot differentiate between the part of her that says, "Don't do it, you will fail," and the part of her that says, "I can't stand another year stuck in this rut." The level of distress is interpreted as a warning against taking action, and before she knows it, she has put away her plans for another day. While she is immobilised by her fear, she continues to maintain the status quo of her life, and cannot make adaptive changes led by her deepest needs. Her fears coupled with her lack of confidence in her ability to achieve her goals block her from connecting with the meaning in her longing.

Reflection 1

- *As a child, how did you learn to manage your vulnerable feelings?*
- *What did you learn about your emotional world as a result? Was it something scary that was best avoided or dealt with alone, or something overwhelming that you could not handle on your own?*
- *Did you learn that your feelings were okay and that others would be there to help you with them?*
- *Or did you learn that your feelings should be pushed away and dealt with alone?*
- *Or that you could not manage your feelings without another's help?*

Reflection 2

As an adult, what do you notice about the way that you manage your emotions?

- *Do you tend to become overwhelmed by the intensity of your emotions?*
- *Or do you tend to suppress, dismiss, or brush over your emotions?*
- *What do you tell yourself about your emotions that could be missing the meaning in them (e.g., emotions are pointless/ scary/harmful)?*
- *Do you tell yourself that they are silly and best ignored?*
- *Or do you tell yourself that they are too big to handle on your own?*

Noticing your own pattern of emotion regulation

Even if you are lucky enough to have learned and developed some secure attachment strategies, times of stress, such as losing someone special to you, can test your capacity for riding the wave of your emotional storms. If, like many people, your earliest attachment figures were not accessible, responsive, and engaged, or if they were unreliable or unsafe, then this will have impacted your ability to manage your emotions. Each frustrating, disappointing, rejecting, anxiety-provoking interaction with a caregiver early in life would have raised valid doubts for you about the point of reaching out to others, and about your own worthiness of love and support. The sad consequence of this type of negative experience is that we seem to internalise the messages we receive from our attachment figures, even if they are really unhelpful to us. This not only impacts how you see yourself, but it also impacts how you interact with your vulnerable emotions throughout your life.

As humans, we tend to treat ourselves the same way that our attachment figures treated us. If you have generally received sensitive caregiving from trustworthy attachment figures, you are likely to treat yourself with the same sensitivity and care. Conversely, if you have experienced your attachment figures to be unreliable and disappointing or even rejecting, you are more likely to treat yourself in this way as well. Left alone to manage your own emotional distress, the only model you have to follow is the one modelled to you. If your caregiver dismissed your vulnerable emotions, you might do this to yourself and others as an adult. If your caregivers were always so far away that you had to amplify your signals of need to reach them, you will do that with yourself and others as an adult. Understanding how you have learned to greet and work with your inner world is key to being able to change those patterns and "earn" security with yourself.

Often, the way we interpret and respond to our emotions, especially those that are negative, can serve to increase and even maintain their negative impact in our life. Discovering how you might bring about and maintain your own negative emotions in self-perpetuating feedback loops can be a revelation or a disruption to the status quo. If you recall our discussion in Chapter 2 about the repetitive and predictable cycles that partners can become stuck in, this is the same process, but it is within yourself. We are looking for the self-perpetuating feedback loops that you might get tangled in with your own emotional experiences. Wretchedly, your best attempt to manage your emotions, in the way that you have been taught in life, might actually be causing you more harm than good. These patterns might be causing you to feel your emotions "too much" or "not enough," and could block you from growth. When we can track these patterns and notice how you might turn up certain emotional experiences or turn down certain emotional experiences, we can then see if these ways of coping with emotions are helping you or hindering you. If they are not helping you to listen to the meaning in your emotion, and to send clear signals to those who matter to you, then we can change them.

Noticing how you might turn towards or turn away from your own inner experiences is the first step in this process. People might turn towards or amplify parts of their inner experience by going back over painful memories, searching for answers that cannot be found, ruminating in a way that only makes them feel worse, focusing on their own or someone else's shortcomings and blaming or criticising, repeatedly focusing on what has gone wrong and how nothing will ever be the same again, looking at their ex-partner's social media to churn over how happy their life appears and to compare it to their own. If you notice yourself doing any of these or similar things, then that is a clue that you might benefit from being able to achieve more *distance* from the intensity of your emotions to be able to hear the message in them. You can see how the more you focus on the most painful and hopeless aspects of a loss, the more you are likely to feel sad and angry and to get stuck there. This will impact how you adjust to the loss, making it harder to let go of the past relationship, and blocking you from embracing new opportunities. The lack of new opportunities then contributes to you looking back at the painful past. In this way, you can remain stuck in a self-perpetuating feedback loop where your best effort to manage your reactive, painful emotions actually makes them worse.

Alternatively, people might turn away from their emotional experiences by not thinking about painful things such as the past too much at all, by disengaging from anything that might stir up emotional feelings for them, by brushing away other people's emotions or offers of help, by focusing only on the practical tasks of life, and by dismissing their vulnerable feelings or even criticising them. The more you push your vulnerable feelings away, the more you miss opportunities to learn from the wisdom of your own experience. The more you cope alone, the more you miss opportunities for co-regulation with a safe other who could show you that closeness can, in fact, be helpful. You can then rob yourself of the most energy-efficient and rewarding way of regulating emotions, co-regulating. If you can see yourself in any of these examples, then that is a clue that you might need to work on *tuning into* your emotional world more.

It is my hope that you can begin to see how you might be interacting with your emotions so that you can see if you are stuck in a pattern like this. **What we can see we can name, what we can name we can understand, and what we can understand we can learn from, and most importantly, change.** The key to changing these patterns is honest observation – holding a mirror up to your experience. As I have mentioned many times throughout this book, once we understand the function in our coping strategies and the meaning in our inner world, then we have found the "gold" in our experience that tells us everything we need to know about what matters most, and what we are crying out for. This can be difficult, but it is always informative!

Reflection 3

Now take a moment to reflect on what we have covered so far; how you learned to interact with your emotions growing up, how that might have changed in your adult relationships, and how you are interacting with your emotions as you process this important loss.

- *Are you becoming stuck in unhelpful patterns of emotional regulation?*
- *What do you need to do to break out of these patterns?*
- *Do you need to get better at gaining a working distance from your painful emotions so you can hear their message?*
- *Or do you need to get better at tuning into your emotions to find the meaning in them?*

How to regulate your emotions effectively

As mentioned earlier in this chapter, there are two important parts to successful emotional regulation. The first is being able to self-soothe, and the second is being able to seek support from others as needed. Both of these skills start with befriending your inner world. This means leaning into your emotional experience rather than pulling back from it. It also means maintaining a working distance from the painful emotions so that you can find the meaning in your experience, rather than being swept away by it.

1. Gaining working distance from your emotions

Let's start by looking at how to self-regulate, or how to "tap the brakes" on your emotional storms if they feel "too much." Being able to do this will help you to ride the waves without bursting through your window of tolerance.[8] Remember the idea of a window of tolerance for being with your emotional world? This is the idea that we all have a natural ability for being with our internal world, but if we think of it as a window, the wider the window, the more emotional highs and lows you can handle without it becoming too much and exceeding your coping ability. The narrower the window, the more quickly we become thrown off-balance by our emotions. We can stretch and widen our window of tolerance by spending more time in contact with our inner world, but we need to do this gradually. Knowing whether you are in your window of tolerance, or if you have burst out the other side, is really important. We do this by staying self-aware and looking out for our coping strategies. When we are reaching for our coping strategies of turning the heat up or down on our emotions, we know we are right at the edge of our window of tolerance and need to pull back. For instance, if Prue becomes aware that she stops planning her overseas adventure the moment her fear about bad things happening gets too high, then she can learn to attune to her levels of fear and can work to bring them down before she gives up planning. Her *old* coping strategy of turning up the heat on her fear (to scare herself out of taking a risk) is her signal that she needs to stay longer with her emotions while not stoking the fear with catastrophic thinking. Therefore, her *new* coping strategy involves tapping the brakes on her fear so that it doesn't get overwhelming, blocking forward movement.

This is what I mean by "tapping the brakes" on intense emotional experiences. When you notice yourself approaching the limits of your window of tolerance, some practical examples for tapping the brakes are: breathing slowly and evenly to calm your nervous system; noticing your intense emotions and mindfully observing the sensations that accompany them; pressing your feet into the floor; noticing things you can see, hear, feel, and smell; and being aware of your thoughts while distancing from them. It can be very helpful to get to know the thoughts that typically show up when you are feeling intense emotion. These represent the meaning that you are making about your emotion, and sometimes they can make things worse. Meaning coming from *reactive* emotion is usually not all that helpful, but meaning that comes from *primary* emotion is extremely helpful. Knowing the difference can be particularly beneficial. Back to Prue, if she tells herself that her intensely fearful feelings are providing evidence that travelling is too dangerous and best avoided, then the meaning she is making goes directly against her core need to seek adventure and growth. If she can tap the brakes on her intense (reactive) fear a little, the meaning connected to her primary emotions and core needs might be able to be heard. Her primary emotions of sadness and curiosity have so much to tell her about her distress that she is not living in line with her core need – to spread her wings and test herself in life. This is the part of her that is telling her how important it is for her to challenge herself, and how bad stifling her life feels currently. When she can connect with this deeper meaning, it drives a completely different course of action that is in line with her needs and values, rather than her reactive fear.

2. Channelling supportive others

Treating yourself with care and compassion is very helpful in tempering intense emotions. As we know, this is easier to do if you have been shown how by caring attachment figures. With repetition, positive interactions with responsive attachment figures help us to form a stable sense of self, which means a sense of who you are, how you feel, what you need, and where you are going. We only need one accessible, responsive, and engaged person in our life growing up to develop, at least, an experience of security. There may have been a teacher, a friend, a coach, a neighbour, a grandparent, or a therapist who gave you a glimpse of a safe connection. This experience not only becomes a blueprint for finding more relationships like this throughout life, but it also shows you how to provide that same care for yourself. This leads to a positive self-identity, through the development of a bank of memories of the other as supportive of you, that you can draw from in uncertain moments. Their positive view of you becomes part of you, and you start to see yourself through their eyes as lovable, capable, and worthy of support. In this way, a piece of this special other is carried around with you and can sustain you without their actual presence.

Amazingly, by thinking about yourself in the way that a cherished attachment figure saw or sees you, and by *imagining* them providing you with support when you need it, you can draw upon their support to give yourself comfort and reassurance when you need it. In this way, you can soothe yourself by bringing a positive person to mind and channelling their love and support. You wouldn't think that someone living or passed could have an impact on us by proxy, but studies show that simply thinking about an attachment figure in times of stress can lower heart rate,[9] reduce markers of stress in saliva,[10] and provide a protection from fear-inducing events.[11] That's pretty marvellous.

A lovely lady told me a story one day about how this helped her, and she allowed me to share it with you. Patricia was driving on a busy road in her small car when a truck wavered into her lane scraping her car and very nearly causing a serious accident. She managed the glancing blow and gestured for the truck driver's attention. As he was slowing to pull over, she noticed that her own reactive fear-response was up and running. With adrenaline pumping, she was ready and primed for a fight, she wanted to scream and cry and rage at this careless driver who threatened her life! In those few moments, as they slowed and stopped the two vehicles, Patricia noticed her reactive fear and made a decision to be a resource to herself in this time of need. She breathed slowly to calm her body and she brought to mind her favourite aunt who was a source of immeasurable love and support to her growing up. She imagined her aunt there with her, soothing her.

She imagined how her aunt might deal with this situation and remembered a similar incident where her aunt was calm and magnanimous. As Patricia saw in her mind's eye, her aunt's loving presence and her calm approach to the problem, Patricia felt centred, her fear reduced to a manageable level and she was able to step out of the car saying to the truck driver "Oh dear, what happened? I can only assume you didn't see me!" Of course, this approach invited openness from the driver who was also shaken. Together, they could work to resolve the situation without reproach or defensiveness.

3. Self-compassion

Compassion occurs when you allow another's suffering into your heart rather than ignoring it or avoiding it. We can learn to be our own safe place by giving ourselves this same consideration and care. Self-compassion involves being kind and understanding towards yourself in moments of pain or failure, rather than being harshly self-critical or judgemental.[12] In this way, we can be touched by our own suffering, and can meet our own experience with gentleness. When we can give this gift of compassion to ourselves, feelings of kindness and caring can emerge. We can genuinely desire our own well-being and can be a resource to ourselves in a time of need. When we bring equanimity and understanding to our appraisal of our mistakes or failings, we can then be open and curious in order to learn from these experiences. We are not talking about indulging ourselves here, we are talking about being kind and not becoming absorbed in negative experiences. We are talking about providing ourselves with compassion and care so that we can dust ourselves off and keep moving towards our goals. Just as a caring parent does when their child hurts themselves in the playground, their compassion and care enable the child to return to play and exploration more quickly – a quick top-up and then they are on their way.

Self-compassion also involves seeing your suffering as part of a bigger human experience, one that connects you to people rather than isolating you from others. We all know what it is like to suffer; you are not alone. The ability to see our suffering as part of a bigger human experience actually *requires* that you step outside of your experience. This means that you cannot help but gain a sense of perspective and working distance from the intensity of the pain. This not only unites you with a collective human experience but also allows you to step back from the intensity of your inner world. To give ourselves care, we have to take the position of "other," which can break a cycle of being absorbed by our emotions. When you can do this, it means that you can now pay attention to your pain without ignoring it *and* you can offer yourself comfort from a working distance.

How do you give yourself love and compassion when you need it? This process starts with noticing your pain, then with acknowledging it and offering yourself kindness in the same way you would offer this to a loved one. Some people naturally offer themselves physical comfort by placing their hands on their chest, wrapping their arms around themselves, or holding their own hand. Offering yourself emotional comfort can be helpful as well. The way you speak to yourself when you are vulnerable and in pain is crucial. Try saying to yourself something like, "I know you are hurting, this is so hard, I'm here with you, you can get through this, you are going to be okay, this will pass." These words of compassion can provide comfort in moments of need and might represent a completely different way of being with yourself and your emotions. In this way, you are becoming your own safe haven and secure base.

4. Finding the meaning in your emotions

Now that you have some tools for managing the intensity of your emotional experiences, it is also important that you are able to tune into your emotions to listen to the wisdom within them. Attending to your emotional experience, in order to process it effectively, means leaning into it in such a way that you can assemble the pieces of this experience into a coherent whole. This means paying attention to your emotional world, and as my wise mentor and friend Kathryn Rheem described it, "befriending" your inner world. She said that just as we get to know a friend, we start as an acquaintance with a vague knowledge of this new person, and then as we are interested in getting to know them more, we lean closer with curiosity. As we discover more about them, we start to understand this new friend, and we develop a connection and affinity with them. We start to understand who they are, to like them more, and to want the best for them. This is how we can treat our own emotional experiences. As though you are learning more about a good friend, except that friend is you.[13]

You might recall working through the process of tuning into our emotions in Chapters 4 and 5. Remember, when we can be with our pain and hold ourselves gently and without judgement, then the emotion can do its work. If we stay with it and allow it to be there, then the emotion will begin to transform. The intensity naturally shrinks as we allow the emotion to unfold and to clarify. This enables you to move into and through it, discovering the wisdom in it as you do so. This wisdom and meaning tells you what you want and need at your deepest levels, and this knowledge becomes a compass-heading for your direction in life.

Reflection 4

- *When your emotions flare, how is it for you to allow that pain, to notice it, and to be with it? Do you find their intensity overwhelming, or do you tend to dismiss them?*
- *What are you learning that you could do to stay within your window of tolerance (i.e., tuning into your emotions more, or gaining working distance from them)?*
- *When you are vulnerable and hurting, what are you discovering that you most need from yourself?*

5. Turning to others when needed

As we know, the most efficient and adaptive way of regulating our emotions is in co-regulation with a safe other. Successful management of our emotions involves being able to self-regulate *and* co-regulate. We have looked at some ways to notice the way you interact with your emotions in your internal world, so that you can work on improving your ability to *self-regulate*. This is of particular importance when you have lost an attachment figure and are having to redirect your attachment needs. There will inevitably be a period of time where you feel adrift and alone as part of processing this separation. As a result, being able to self-regulate might be especially required at the moment. While self-regulation is really important, reaching out to *others* when we need them is also how we regulate our emotions. As part of adjusting to the loss of such a significant attachment relationship, you will need to consider being able to turn to others for your attachment needs, especially now that your ex-partner is no longer the one you can turn to first. This might mean building new connections with others or strengthening existing ones. It is important to make a concerted effort to ensure that you have some safe others to lean on as a resource. We all need support from people who matter to us, and seeing that no one can be our "everything," it is sensible to have multiple attachment figures you can call upon when you need them.

The good news is that all your hard work to tune into your emotional world, and to bring kindness to your experience, will significantly alter the way that you signal your needs to those who matter to you. This means that you are going to naturally be much clearer about what you want and need from your special people than you otherwise might have been. The clarity of your signals increases the chance of others responding positively to you, and of your needs being met. This is the positive benefit of secure attachment strategies. When you can tune into yourself and understand what it is that you are needing, then it is much easier to know who might be able to meet those needs or provide the comfort you are seeking. When you are clear about what you need, you will send much clearer signals to your attachment figures, making it much easier for them to meet your needs effectively. To build further on this idea, in our final chapter, we are going to look at how to take all this wonderful security into your next close or romantic relationship.

Chapter 7 takeaways

- Emotions perform several crucial functions that enhance our well-being and maintain our social connections; they provide us with information about our internal and external worlds, they direct our attention to our needs, they motivate us to act according to our needs and values, and they help us to connect with others.
- Being able to engage with our own internal emotional world, rather than ignoring or denying parts of it, is key in finding the meaning in our experience.
- Regulating our emotions involves being able to self-regulate (self-soothe) and to co-regulate (turn to others when we need them). It involves being able to listen to our emotional signals, *and* it means being able to temporarily shelve them when needed. The art of self-regulation is proficiency at *tuning into* your emotions when needed, *and* gaining *working distance* from them when needed.
- We learn how to regulate our emotions in our earliest attachment relationships, and this ability continues to develop in every meaningful relationship we have throughout our life.

- The attachment strategies you use impact the way you interact with and manage your emotions. People with *secure* attachment strategies tend to be relatively unafraid of their emotions and are able to self-regulate and learn from their emotions, as well as turn to others as needed. People with *avoidant* attachment strategies learn to suppress, avoid, and deny their emotions, to not rely on others, and therefore can miss the meaning in their emotional signals. People with *anxious* attachment strategies are likely to have little confidence in their ability to manage their emotions without the help of a trusted other, and can become overwhelmed in their intensity, potentially missing the meaning in their experience.
- Just like negative patterns between partners, we can become stuck in negative patterns with our own emotions. Sometimes, our best attempt to manage our painful emotions can serve to block us from finding the meaning in them.
- Some tips to regulate your emotions include gaining a working distance from your intense emotions by staying within your window of tolerance, calling an attachment figure to mind, treating yourself with compassion, tuning into the meaning embedded in your emotion, and reaching out to others when you need them.
- Being able to self-regulate means that when you need to turn to a safe other for co-regulation, you are going to send clearer, more coherent signals of vulnerability and need, which makes it easier for them to be a resource for you.

Notes

1. Frijda, N. H. (1986). *The emotions.* Cambridge: Cambridge University Press.
2. Johnson, S. M. (2019). *Attachment theory in practice: Emotionally focused therapy (EFT) with individuals, couples and families.* New York: The Guilford Press.
3. Bowlby, J. (1991). Postscript. In C. M. Parkes, J. Stevenson-Hinde, & P. Marris (Eds.), *Attachment across the lifespan* (pp. 293–297). New York: Routledge.
4. Porges, S. W. (2011). *Polyvagal theory: Neurophysiological foundations of emotions, attachment, communication, and self-regulation.* New York: W.W. Norton & Company, Inc.
5. Greenberg, L. (2008). Emotion and cognition in psychotherapy: The transforming power of affect. *Canadian Psychology, 49*(1), 40–59.

6. Shaver, P. R., & Mikulincer, M. (2016). *Attachment in adulthood: Structure, dynamics and change* (2nd ed.). New York: The Guilford Press.
7. Cozolino, L. (2014). *The neuroscience of human relationships: Attachment and the developing social brain* (2nd ed.). New York: W.W. Norton & Company, Inc.
8. Siegel, D. J. (1999). *The developing mind.* New York: The Guilford Press.
9. Bryant, R. A., & Hutanamon, T. (2018). Activating attachment enhances heartrate variability. *PLOS ONE, 13*(2): e0151747.
10. Bryant, R. A., & Chan, L. (2015). Thinking of attachments reduces noradrenergic stress response. *Psychoneuroendocrinology, 60,* 39–45.
11. Toumbelekis, M., Liddell, B. J., & Bryant, R. A. (2018). Thinking of attachment figures blocks differential fear conditioning. *Social Cognitive and Affective Neuroscience, 13*(9), 989–994.
12. Neff, K. (2004). Self-compassion and psychological wellbeing. *Constructivism in the Human Sciences, 9*(2), 27–37.
13. Rheem, K., & Olden, J. (2021). The EFT Cafe. Office hours, March 2021. www.theeftcafe.com

EIGHT

Building security in future relationships

We have arrived! Here we are at the final chapter of this book. You have bravely come with me on this winding path of discovery where you have strived to get to know yourself as an attachment-driven being, where you have been willing to hold a mirror up to your emotional experience and humbly take responsibility for that which you are least proud. You have processed big feelings and hopefully grown stronger by encountering your own resilience and the exquisite wisdom in your pain. You have bravely journeyed through the lowest of lows to find meaning and growth in this major life event. It is my most sincere hope that you are feeling more steady and better able to let go of this past relationship so that you can start to look forward to creating the future you want.

In this chapter, we now look at how to bring your insights about your past relationships, your attachment strategies, and your emotional awareness into your next relationship. To start this process, we will explore the beliefs you might be carrying with you, from the past, about close relationships. Then, I will help you to bravely walk back onto the playing field of romantic love with your inner security waving like a banner. We will investigate how to detect secure attachment strategies in others to ensure that you set off on the right foot. You can *now* create the relationship you want, so we will focus on *how* to shape the security that you are seeking in your new emotional bonds. We will take all you have learned about yourself and your deepest needs and help you to honour these as you consider entering a new relationship. We will look at how to spot and avoid unhelpful dynamics in relationships, and how to earn security together as you create a loving bond with someone special.

DOI: 10.4324/9781003264163-12

Mental representations and expectations of others

We all hold beliefs about the value of close relationships and our fundamental lovability. These can either help or hinder our attempts to find love. As you work to release yourself from the emotional ties to your ex-partner and look towards the idea of embarking on new connections moving forward, it might pay to be aware of the expectations or biases about relationships you could be carrying with you. Sometimes, these expectations can become self-fulfilling prophecies that, without our awareness, can live on unchallenged within us, and can cause us to perpetuate past negative patterns in future relationships. This is common unless we pause and understand ourselves and others. I don't want that for you, so the aim of the first part of this chapter is to help you to identify the beliefs you might be holding about relationships and your self-worth that could impact the quality of your future attachment bonds.

As we have already illustrated, our attachment strategies don't just impact how we interact with others and how we manage our own emotions, they also impact our belief systems about relationships. Our social experiences with attachment figures early in life provide a foundation for our subsequent attachment relationships throughout the rest of our life. Our lived experiences of turning to our attachment figures during times of need offer powerful learnings that we store away in the form of "working models."[1] As we discussed in Chapter 3, we have two key working models that relate to our attachment needs, they are a *model of other* and a *model of self*. These models provide a template or set of expectations for what it means to turn to another in times of need, and what we can expect from this (model of other) as well as about our own self-worth and lovability (model of self). Being aware of your own thoughts and expectations in close relationships is extremely helpful in getting to know yourself better, and represents the first step in being able to move out of old relational patterns when your attachment alarms go off (as they inevitably do for us all).

The attachment strategies a person tends to use, and their working models, play important roles in the expectations they have about love and attachment, their beliefs about their own self-worth, and in their perception of other people's intentions and trustworthiness. We know from previous research that people with *secure* attachment strategies have a generally optimistic view of love and relationships, and a positive sense of self.

Because they have experienced their caregivers as sensitive and responsive, they are likely to form positive beliefs about close relationships, and to have developed a healthy sense of self. They bring these open and positive ideas with them into their relationships, which means that they are more likely to see their partner in a positive light, to feel confident about their partner's reliability, and to feel worthy of love and support. We can expect people with secure attachment strategies to see their partner's transgressions in a more understanding light, and to be accepting and encouraging of their partner without feeling inadequate or needing constant approval or reassurance.[2] These positive views of self and other are likely to set up supportive and helpful experiences of reaching openly, sharing honestly, and giving and receiving encouragement and care, all of which create compounding and self-reinforcing patterns between partners.

Given that people with *anxious* attachment strategies are likely to have experienced their caregivers as inconsistently available, they are likely to hold more complex or even negative views of other's reliability in their adult relationships, and to doubt their own lovability. Sadly, people with anxious attachment strategies are quite susceptible to blaming themselves for their attachment figures' lack of reliability, and so tend to believe that if they put more effort into catching their important other's attention and approval, then they will be successful in acquiring their love and support. Despite their fears of abandonment and self-doubt, people who use anxious attachment strategies remain hopeful about the potential of love to soothe them. They will generally believe that it is easy to fall in love, and that this is a regular occurrence. Therefore, they can carry with them confusing beliefs about others, where they see their attachment figure as the solution to their vulnerability, and hold hope that they will be responsive to their needs, and they also carry doubt about the other's reliability and their own worthiness of love. Of course, their partner will not always be able to be responsive to them, so these beliefs are bound to be confirmed at least some of the time, adding fuel to the fire of fear about impending rejection or abandonment. Furthermore, their way of expressing their heightened fears can play a role in the other's lack of responsiveness, as we discussed in Chapter 2 when looking at negative cycles that partners can become tangled up in.

People with *avoidant* attachment strategies are more likely to doubt that romantic love happens, or even exists. They carry with them more cynical beliefs about relationships, and pre-emptively conclude that others cannot be relied on, and do not have positive intentions. This arises from the cumulative effect of experiencing their early caregivers as rejecting or dismissive of their attachment needs. They have learned that it is better to cope alone, and to suppress their painful emotions, rather than risk turning to an unresponsive or rejecting caregiver. As adults, people with avoidant attachment strategies are not likely to take their emotional needs to another, or even to acknowledge them to themselves. In so doing, they may miss opportunities to learn from their emotional world and can skip over opportunities for a partner to disprove this belief system with their responsiveness and care. In this way, people with avoidant attachment strategies might even miss genuine signals of support or connection coming from their partner, or only pay them a passing glance which can rob them of an opportunity to disprove or alter their working model of other. As a result, their pessimistic views of love and connection live on disproven, and their self-reliant coping goes on unchallenged.

Reflection 1

I hope that it is becoming a little clearer how the beliefs we bring with us into our close relationships can become self-perpetuating, often without our conscious awareness. Take a moment to reflect on the beliefs that you might be carrying with you into your next close relationship.

- *What beliefs do you carry with you about the value of close relationships?*
- *What do you see as the benefit of turning to another in times of emotional need?*
- *What do you feel that you deserve to receive in your close relationships?*

Bringing security into a new relationship

Coming to understand where and what you learned about relationships and your own worth means that you are taking important steps in building your self-awareness. As we know, self-awareness involves tuning into your inner world, *and* zooming out to see the bigger patterns in your life. It means listening to your deepest needs, and intentionally letting them guide your life direction and your interactions with others. Knowing yourself in this way allows you to be a resource for yourself, and to draw on others as a resource as well. It lets you know when you have stepped away from what matters to you, or when you might be playing a role in the blocking of your needs. This awareness is key to being able to intentionally make changes for the better.

If you take a moment to reflect on the work you have done so far in this book, it is clear to me that you have been contributing towards the growth of your attachment security, and that is a big step. It is my hope that becoming aware of your attachment strategies has helped you to see how they might have impacted the way you have shown up in relationships and built an awareness of what might have been missing for you in your earliest attachment relationships, as well as your adult relationships. Now that you can see that the way you have been attempting to get your needs met in close relationships might have actually contributed to some of the insecurity in your previous bond, then you know what to work on in future relationships to take responsibility for your half of the connection. The way you have been exploring and working through the pain of the loss of your past relationship will have set you in good stead for detaching from this bond and redefining this past relationship. This means that you can now be open to new connections, unencumbered by unresolved feelings and yearnings. In this way, you have stemmed the bleeding and cared for the wound yourself, thereby discovering your capacity for self-care. By dedicating time to the reading of this book, you have already stepped into new territory. This new territory involves greeting your pain with openness and compassion, reflecting on how you communicate your needs to others, and understanding yourself as an attachment being.

When looking at how to take this inner wisdom into your next close relationship, I believe that tuning into your inner world is the best place to start. The process of being able to listen closely to your own emotions, rather than ignoring or avoiding them or becoming deafened or swallowed up by them, is instrumental in being able to interact differently with yourself, and to connect fully with your deepest wants and needs. When you can greet yourself in your most vulnerable moments with compassion and gentleness, and when you can soothe and sustain yourself with encouragement, then you are giving yourself a wonderful gift. This is a secure way of being with yourself – providing yourself with a safe haven and a secure base. When we can treat ourselves with kindness and understanding, we will feel worthy of this from others as well. When we can soothe the parts that hurt, it is easier to ask for what we need from others in a more clear and coherent way. This allows us to take in loving messages and feel the full benefit of another's care and responsiveness. When we know ourselves and our pain, we can walk with it differently, and we can *signal* our needs to others in ways that pull them close rather than alienating them and leaving ourselves isolated.

When we can treat ourselves in this supportive way, and we can signal our needs or vulnerabilities clearly to a safe other, it invites them to come closer and allows them the opportunity of being your safe place. When this happens, when someone can be accessible and responsive to you in a time of need, and you can let that care in and receive it, your bond gets stronger. This sets up a beautiful pattern of reaching and responding, of reciprocal risk and acceptance of each other that defines secure attachment. This process starts with two people who care about each other, who are willing to let each other see into their inner world and treat what they find there with gentleness and acceptance. Your role in this is to bring compassion and kindness to yourself, and an open heart to the other. If you can risk letting another see into your heart in small ways, and they can do the same, then you are *fearlessly loving*.

Another secret to leading with security in your next close rela-tionship is to zoom out and see the bigger picture of how you interact with those who matter most to you (and how you interact with yourself) as this can be eye-opening. Without awareness of self-defeating patterns, a person can live on oblivious to the ways their assumptions and expectations are being brought to life and how their best attempts to cope with discomfort might actually be contributing to their dissatisfaction. Seeing these patterns between yourself and those who matter, and the patterns you might get caught in within your inner world, is revelatory. As we have said, *what you can see and feel, you can name, what you can name, you can understand, and what you can understand, you can change.* Being able to see and alter the way you approach close relation-ships, and your own inner world, has been the bulk of your emo-tional labour so far in this book.

Knowing your relational raw spots, and how you usually react when they are pressed, is crucial in this process. If you think back to our discussions about negative cycles in relationships, and you reflect on what things your partner did or didn't do that triggered attachment alarms for you, what do you recall was your go-to knee-jerk response? If you are like most of us, it was something that made complete sense to you, but sent scary signals to the other person that set off *their* sirens and alarms, and before you knew it, you were both stuck in your *negative cycle*. I know that you have worked so hard to understand your own reactions and sensitivities since then, and you can now see what softer, more tender emotions (primary emotions) might have been lurking underneath the defensive, reactive positions you might have taken in those "old" patterns. However, holding this in your mind now is important so that you can be watchful for this faithful, if no longer helpful, coping strategy reappearing. Typically, these coping strategies have been learned for good reason in earlier times in your life and will remain loyal to you even when they are no longer required. That old urge to retreat into your protective shell, or to lash out to guard yourself from harm, will hopefully not be required if you can shape the relationship that you want; one where you do not need to protect yourself or chase love, where you feel safe and cherished and accepted.

Knowing and *catching* your faithful coping strategy (attachment strategy) in action is very important to being able to intentionally show up with a new partner in a more secure way. For instance, if you have learned that you can shut down and become very logical if a partner is hurt or disappointed by you, then catching this "old" way of coping is vital to being able to take a different path in a new relationship. You might instead offer yourself some soothing by saying "I know it is hard when I have upset my partner, this means that I care, it doesn't mean that I'm being rejected as I have been in the past, I can best repair this connection by showing that I care about their hurt and not shutting down." This kind, but firm, way of reminding yourself of your decision to be more emotionally present with yourself and your new partner is helpful in holding yourself to account and ensuring that you walk a new path. Alternatively, if you know that your coping strategy (attachment strategy) is to escalate your demands of your partner when you sense their distance, you can catch yourself catastrophising in your mind and self-soothe by breathing slowly and calmly, and saying something to yourself like "I am scared because I have been let down in the past, but I am safe now, I can share my fear in soft ways, I don't need to get loud to be heard, my partner will hear me because they care."

This soothing and reassuring presence validates that you have a good reason for your fear, and it also reminds you that you can share it in new ways that invite a different response from your special person. This is how you can intentionally use secure attachment strategies.

Another important part of bringing security into your next relationship is not losing sight of what matters to you in favour of the other person, or the relationship. This means not disconnecting from your inner world that informs you about your deepest fears, needs, goals, and values. Staying tuned into your emotional signalling system is crucial to maintaining your emotional balance, and not veering away from what is important to you as a person. This actually takes conscious effort and practice, and believe me, I understand, it can be hard. Remaining connected to yourself requires regularly listening and asking yourself how you are feeling and what you are needing, and it involves knowing your vulnerabilities and tendencies. For instance, you might be the kind of person who prioritises the other's happiness above your own in a relationship, and so tend to bend too far and give up things that matter to you for the good of the other. Alternatively, you might fear losing yourself in a relationship, and so tend to express your wants and needs in rigid and uncompromising ways that risk damaging the bond.

Staying connected to your own experience means listening to that inner voice that reminds you of what really matters to you, and it means not silencing the warning voice inside that tells you when your needs are at risk of being neglected. For instance, this warning might flare if a relationship could be demanding too much sacrifice from you or taking you in a direction that leads away from your core needs and values. While we all have to be willing to compromise to fit our lives and dreams with another's, listening to your own emotional signalling system will be invaluable in assuring that your voice is heard, and that your needs are not squashed. Tuning in like this is key to maintaining a connection with yourself. It will also allow you to remain more attentive to your partner's needs.

As you ponder this, it might be worth reflecting on what you need to hold yourself to account for in your next relationship. What I mean by this is making a commitment to yourself to work on how you show up in your next relationship, how you are going to remain tuned into your emotional world, and how you are going to consciously manage your reactive emotions differently.

I am asking you to hold yourself to account for your own core needs and values, and make a promise to yourself that these will not fade into the background of your awareness when you become swept up in a new love, or out of fear of being alone. Determine and honour your "non-negotiables" when it comes to your next close relationship. Rather than making this an exhaustive list of desirable traits in a prospective partner, think about the things that might not align with your needs and values. In this way, you are being your own best friend who only wants the best for you, and who would never want you to lose sight of that which nourishes and fulfils you. This is particularly important in the early stages of a new relationship where there is likely to be the "golden glow" of new love that has been called limerence.[3] In this exciting stage, it is extremely easy to gloss over small issues, and to lose connection with yourself.

Reflection 2

In thinking about how you would like to show up in your next close relationship, I would like to ask you to write a letter to yourself. This letter represents a commitment to yourself, and I ask that you write it in a loving and compassionate tone, just as you would speak to a cherished friend. Be sure to take the following questions into account as you write this pledge to yourself:

- *What do I need to do to ensure that I remain connected to myself, to my emotions and needs?*
- *How can remind myself to check-in with myself and to listen to my inner signals?*
- *How can I treat my pain and vulnerability with love and compassion?*
- *What is my "old" coping strategy that I need to curb? How will I know when it shows up?*
- *What do I need to do differently to take a new path (to lead with secure strategies)?*
- *What are my non-negotiables in my next relationship?*
- *What important needs and values do I promise not to lose sight of in the whirlwind of a new love, or out of fear of being alone?*

Keep this somewhere safe, hold it close, and read it often. It is the whisperings of your deepest needs from the person who knows you most and wants nothing but the best for you.

Looking for secure attachment strategies in another

I once had a light-hearted chat with a friend about how she could be sure that she picked a partner with secure attachment strategies for her next big romance. Incidentally, she also happened to be a relationship therapist, so you can imagine what fun we had trying think up methods to "assess" her potential mate's attachment strategies. We thought of lots of ways to put the poor unsuspecting wretch under pressure to see if they responded in an emotionally engaged way, whether they displayed empathic attunement to her feelings should she squeeze out a tear, and whether they would express their own feelings openly. As you can imagine, the picture we painted was not overly attractive for a potential partner to walk into, and my friend wouldn't have been doing herself any favours by behaving in this way. Any self-respecting individual would head for the hills being given such awkward challenges on a first date! And by a relationship therapist no less!

All joking aside, it got me thinking about how one might choose wisely to make sure that their next relationship moves in a different direction from those of the past. What signs might indicate security in a potential partner? I'm wanting to be clear here that I'm not suggesting only people with secure attachment strategies make good partners, or that you should discriminate against those who do not use secure attachment strategies. If that were true, then a huge proportion of society would be relegated to the relationship scrap heap. What a waste! Rather, I am suggesting that you look out for *signs of security* in your potential partner. Their attachment strategies (e.g., the ways they respond to you, how they regulate their emotions, and how they express their attachment needs to another) can be indications that a person is working towards earning security and might offer positive indicators for potentially establishing a secure bond together. Just as you have done, when someone can develop beyond their life circumstances, the learning and self-awareness gained is a great asset moving forwards. Let's look at some signs of security that, if spotted in a potential partner, might enhance your chance of relationship success together.

One thing that stands out to me as a sign of security is when someone is comfortable in their own skin, and they do not speak badly about others, or need to elevate themselves. This is such a lovely quality that shows a quiet self-assurance and a total lack of defensiveness. They are interested in other people because other's successes do not threaten their sense of who they are. Other indicators of security are when a person can both listen and share openly, and as my friend was assessing, when someone can attune empathically to other people's feelings. If someone can see things from perspectives other than their own, and they are open to alternative viewpoints, they demonstrate flexibility in their views and curiosity about things they are still to learn. Individuals with secure attachment strategies are optimistic about love and life, and they are positive about their future and about life's challenges.

Another sign to look out for, which I think is positive in a potential partner, is that they can speak about their past relationships in a way that respects their past loves and reflects a balanced view of why their relationships ended. This might be an indicator not just of security, but also of trauma growth, of learning from adversity. *That* we can certainly admire, knowing what we know about that process! When someone can talk about their flaws and their strengths in an open and balanced way and can also show genuine interest in you as a potential partner, this is a lovely sign. Notice how they attune to you and pick up on your feelings, notice if they are able to acknowledge your strengths as well as "selling themselves" in those early formative experiences together.

Staying tuned into your own emotional signals, while in the presence of a new prospective partner, is very important. Your intuition or "gut feeling" about a person is often very valuable, especially when it is backed up by collateral information (e.g., when friends you trust have the same reaction). Notice whether they spark your curiosity, and whether you feel emotionally safe and understood by them. Observe whether they share their emotion, hopes, and dreams with you, and whether you each are *evenly* disclosing about these sensitive topics. We are aiming for mutual risk and sharing rather than one person doing all the exposing of themselves while the other remains guarded or separate. Beware of any relationship biases or expectations that you could be bringing into this potential relationship and catch them if they are clouding your view of this person. In this way, you are trying to keep balance between tuning into your emotional signals that are giving you valuable information about your safety and about the nature of this emerging connection, but you are also stepping in to curb fears that may not be related to this person at all and could block or rush the development of an authentic bond.

Above all, we must remember that it is normal for fears to come alive when you consider entering into a new close relationship; opening your heart to someone is risky. What you do with those fears can determine if you close your heart, or risk giving it to someone prematurely. *Security is not a prerequisite for having an enriching relationship*, so do not beat yourself up for not having achieved more security within yourself, or judge potential partners for struggling a little on this path either. We are all somewhere on this path, and loving partners can *earn* security together. Developing secure attachment strategies can be a *lifelong process*, and that's totally okay (Rome wasn't built in a day after all).

Earning and shaping security together

Deciding to take the plunge into a close relationship can be both wonderful and terrifying, especially when you are still carrying some emotional bruises from the past. I want to take a moment to explore how to build a bond together, so that you can start out on a great path in your next relationship that will set you up to earn security together. All the good work you have done in understanding your attachment strategies and your deepest needs will help you step into this relationship in new ways. Remember, all partners in close relationships typically need to feel accepted, supported, and understood as well as feeling loved, appreciated, and important. These are such normal needs, and having them met in a healthy and mutually satisfying relationship enhances our physical and mental health.

Building a bond is achieved through mutual sharing and emotional responsiveness. This means opening up to each other and greeting each other with understanding and compassion. As you might recall from earlier chapters, a secure attachment figure is accessible, responsive, and engaged; they are there when you need them, they offer comfort and support, and they care about you. Any time one partner feels uncertain about the other's availability or emotional engagement and their attachment system fires up, if they can take their vulnerable feelings to the other and are greeted with warmth, reassurance, and comfort, then the bond is strengthened. Each time you risk revealing another part of yourself (intentionally or unintentionally) to your partner, and they respond with acceptance and compassion, the more your trust and self-confidence grows. Each time you signal for them in a time of need, and they hear your call and reach back, you know you can rely on them and that you are safe with them. Each time they pick you up when you fall down, the more you know that they are your safe place and your springboard in life (and vice versa). In this way, your attachment bond gradually develops through large and small reaches and risks, leaps of faith that are proven to be safe. These are the ways that secure attachment strategies lead to the building of a secure attachment bond. Moments of connection like this build a sense of trust that the other is dependable, safe, accepting, and responsive.

Security in the attachment bond between close adults means that both share and reveal themselves in roughly equal amounts (not that anyone is keeping score particularly); a bit like going down a staircase together, one step at a time with no one getting too far out in front, and no one being left behind. This means that the bond is reciprocal, both partners have needs, and are needed by the other. When we share like this, both partners experience the rewards of having a secure attachment figure, and both bear a risk of being hurt. When we form a close bond like this with someone special, we are handing our heart to the other, and hoping they don't drop it; each holds the other's heart in their hands. It is a delicate balance of giving and receiving, leaping and being caught. Such is the risk and reward of a loving another deeply and forming a close attachment bond. The more secure the bond, the less risky it is to let yourself wholeheartedly love and be loved.

As you can see, partners in close relationships become each other's attachment figure, and secure attachment means being each other's safe haven and secure base. If you recall us talking about this in earlier chapters, a safe haven is a soft place to land when we feel uncertain, afraid, vulnerable, unwell, or sad; a secure base is a strong and stable platform underneath us to reassure us and encourage us to be brave. Secure partners provide both these functions for each other, and as humans, we need both of these forms of support, from the cradle to the grave.[4] Partners can be a safe haven of comfort for each other in a number of ways, such as listening when the other is worried, caring for the other when they are sick, helping them with a task when they are struggling, asking about their feelings, asking questions about the other's day, providing comfort and concern when the other is hurt, touching them lovingly and affectionately. Partners can act as a secure base in many ways, such as encouraging the other when they doubt themselves, being interested in the other's dreams and goals, providing reassurance when they are uncertain or afraid, expressing belief in the other, helping the other to talk through a problem, supporting the other to get started on a difficult task, acknowledging the other's strengths, and appreciating their efforts. By making sure that you are offering your new partner both a safe haven of comfort and a secure base of support, then you know that you are providing them with something extremely valuable. It is totally appropriate for you to seek these functions from your special person as well. Remember though, it takes time and many repeated experiences of you each meeting these vital needs for the other that builds a secure bond. This is an investment built over time, and what a worthy investment it is.

Reflection 3

- *How could I offer my partner a safe haven when they need it?*
- *How could I show my support and encouragement for my partner's dreams?*
- *How could I treat my partner's vulnerability gently?*
- *What do I need from my partner to feel comforted when I am vulnerable?*
- *How can my partner best support and encourage me when I am uncertain?*
- *How could I signal these needs clearly?*

Getting out of negative patterns that can threaten security

The emotional bond between partners needs to be built with conscious intentionality; it takes effort, care, and attention to nurture a bond of this nature. As we know, this requires sensitive attunement and engagement with yourself and your partner, and it requires the mutual risk of being open with each other. These are secure attachment strategies that will help you to develop a secure bond together. As your new bond is growing, try not to panic if there are hits and misses along the way. The process of coming to interpret each other's signals and understand each other's needs can definitely be bumpy! There is no way you can automatically *know* or intuit exactly what your partner needs on an attachment level. You can take a guess based on what we broadly know humans need to feel securely connected to another, but as you know, this can vary between people depending on their individual encounters with attachment figures throughout their lives. Our particular attachment strategies and our experiences in close relationships impact how we ask for our attachment needs (or not) and the types of things that set off our attachment alarms. When a bond is forming, we *help* the other to be a source of comfort and support by telling them what we are needing, rather than expecting them to just *know*. This is where clear signals of need really help to remove ambiguity. Remember, the more you are paying attention to your own inner emotional world, the more you will know about your deepest fears and needs. This knowledge is invaluable in being able to share clearly with your new partner when it feels right to do so. This way, your partner has the opportunity to help you with those feelings and needs; they can be a resource to you. Even if they cannot change things for you on a practical level, sharing with a safe other in this way breaks the isolation of coping alone.

The sending and receiving of clear emotional signals like this is the most effective way of building a strong bond. It also is an effective way to repair a frayed bond after a moment of disconnection, or a relational hurt. These are moments when the bond is wobbled by the other not being a safe haven or a secure base, such as when one partner might be unaware or not hearing the other's needs, when they might be unavailable to the other in a time of need, when there is an unexpected absence or separation, when there are misunderstandings and mis-attunements, when there are disagreements or disappointments, or when there are breaches of trust. If an attachment bond is like a beautiful silk rope, made of many interwoven threads that give it its strength, then an attachment rupture is an event that tears some of these threads. Ruptures are a normal part of a healthy, secure connection. No relationship can be in perfect resonance and attunement all the time; this is just not possible. In fact, research shows us that security is built through being attuned (in sync with each other) approximately one-third of the time. This means that we can still be securely attached even if we are missing or misinterpreting each other's cues (rupture) and are working to repair and get back into attunement. The process of getting it so right and so wrong with each other is part of the growth of a healthy attachment bond. In fact, ruptures are thought to strengthen the bond between people.[5] For this reason, I suggest greeting ruptures as opportunities for strengthening understanding between you both. Try to see each rupture as adding more threads to your rope together. However, bear in mind that the size of the rupture determines how many of the threads are severed and how long it will take to repair. Small breaks and rips are easier to fix than huge fractures to your bond. The newer the relationship, the more fragile the growing bond, so smaller ruptures early on might have a larger impact than they might once the bond is established and the rope is stronger.

When bids for contact are repeatedly unmet (dismissed, ignored, brushed off, countered, not heard), or partners are frequently out of sync (not understanding what the other needs, in disagreement, sending confusing signals about need, not able to soothe the other), then these moments can create repeated ruptures. Repetitive ruptures can fray the bond that connects partners and can make repair difficult. They raise doubts about the safety of the connection, and about the other's reliability, which can press on sensitive and bruised places in one or both partners. When sensitivities like this are awoken in a new relationship, this sets off attachment alarms, and people can reach for their familiar, "old faithful" (if no longer helpful) attachment strategies. As we know, these "old" coping strategies make sense to the user, but can be triggering to the other, hence setting off escalating patterns of attachment alarm that can develop into negative cycles. The more each partner reacts in their self-protective manner, the scarier they appear to the other, and the more disconnected they become. If you recall from Chapter 2, these negative cycles or patterns can become entrenched and can threaten the attachment bond, making it insecure. If you notice a stuck pattern like this appearing in your new relationship, it is important that you can catch and slow this process so that you can both intentionally step out of defensiveness, and into openness with each other. Getting into an interactional pattern with someone who you care about is inevitable, but shaping how you carry yourself and how clearly you signal your needs in these stuck moments is key to this not becoming a dysfunctional pattern that damages your bond. Below are some ideas for exiting these negative patterns if they start to show up.

Reflection 4

If you find yourself hurt or disappointed by your new partner, ask yourself:

- *How can I share my hurt in non-blaming ways so that they can hear my need?*

- *What do I need to work on to be sure that I send clear and non-triggering signals to my person when I need them?*

If you find yourself in a stuck place with your new partner, take a moment to think about the self-soothing strategies we discussed in Chapter 7 such as breathing slowly, giving yourself compassion and care, connecting with the meaning in your emotional experience, and clarifying your needs and fears. You might need to call a "time-out" on the interaction with your partner if you are both upset or unable to see things flexibly and from the other's perspective. Give yourselves some time to regulate alone (i.e., self-regulation). Make sure that this time apart has a clear end point so that you both know when you will regroup and return to the topic at hand, hopefully in a more engaged and attuned way. Use this time alone to decompress, to "tap the brakes" on extreme emotions and the rigid or helpful thoughts that could be fuelling them. Try to connect with the attachment pain and vulnerability beneath your surface reactive emotions. Ask yourself:

- *What is hurting my heart right now?*
- *How might I be sending my partner frightening signals in my reactive state?*
- *What do I need my special other to know?*
- *What do I need their help with?*
- *What do I need at a deep, primary, heart-level?*
- *How can I offer myself some care and compassion right now?*
- *How could I let them know how I am feeling and what I am needing in a gentle way?*
- *How could I be their safe haven and secure base right now?*
- *How can I calm their nervous system?*

Sharing vulnerably in this way becomes the antidote to disconnection. Vulnerability is the glue that bonds people together.

Celebration

Well, here you are at the very end of this book! It is my most heartfelt hope that you have felt supported as you have worked through the process of honouring your pain, accepting and learning from your loss, and have emerged stronger for this labour. I hope that I have been able to offer you a hand to hold in the dark, and some comfort in your vulnerability. I hope that you are seeing some light now, light that is emanating from your very bright future. I hope that you will take all this knowledge about attachment, relationships, and your beautiful self forward into a life of self-acceptance and secure bonding with the special people in your life. That is my wish for you and for all of us; all imperfect humans trying to find our way with those who matter most to us. Now, instead of looking back to find answers, when you look back, all you'll see is how far you've come. Go and be brave and love fearlessly, you can do it, you deserve it! I only wish I could witness it and celebrate with you!

Chapter 8 takeaways

- We all hold beliefs about the value of close relationships and our fundamental lovability, and these can either help or hinder our attempts to find love. Be aware of yours so that they don't become self-fulfilling prophecies that could block your future connections.
- Generally, people with *secure* attachment strategies have an optimistic view of love and relationships, and a positive sense of self. People with *anxious* attachment strategies are likely to hold more complex or even negative views of other's reliability in their adult relationships, and to doubt their own lovability. People with *avoidant* attachment strategies are more likely to doubt that romantic love happens, or even exists. They carry with them more cynical beliefs about relationships, and preemptively conclude that others cannot be relied on, and do not have positive intentions.
- Self-awareness means greeting your inner emotional world with openness and compassion, reflecting on how you communicate your needs to others, and understanding yourself as an attachment being. Knowing yourself in this way helps you to step into a new relationship in a different way, if you choose to.
- You can lead with security in your next relationship by tuning into your own needs and sending clear signals to the other. Being aware of how you impact the other, and what raw spots or sensitivities you might carry with you, is key in being able to catch "old" coping strategies and choosing to

respond differently. This is how you can intentionally use secure attachment strategies.

- Knowing your tendencies ("old" attachment strategies) when triggered is important in being able to deliberately take a new path in your next close relationship. Be clear about what you need to work on, such as tuning into your emotions or tapping the brakes on the intensity of your experience so that you can send clearer messages to your partner.
- Make a commitment to yourself to remain tuned into your emotional world, and to hold yourself to account for your own core needs and values. Make a promise to yourself that these will not fade into the background of your awareness when you become swept up in a new love, or out of fear of being alone.
- Looking for signs of security in a potential partner such as openness, empathy, interest in others, and non-defensiveness might help you to choose your next partner wisely, and in line with your needs.
- An emotional bond is developed with conscious attention to emotional engagement, and by being a safe haven of comfort and a secure base for each other.
- Ruptures are a normal part of healthy attachment development and maintenance, and the size of the rupture impacts the ease of repair.
- Repeated ruptures and misalignments can press on sensitivities for partners and can trigger "old" ways of coping. These can set off escalating patterns of attachment alarm that can develop into negative cycles. Negative cycles can threaten the attachment bond.
- Catching and exiting these stuck patterns is important in preventing them from becoming entrenched and damaging your bond.
- You can exit negative interactional patterns by using these secure attachment strategies:
  o Taking time away from the conflict to self-soothe, and to reflect on what you are needing and feeling at a deep, primary level before regrouping.
  o Signalling your needs and fears clearly and in a non-blaming/non-defensive way, with vulnerability and openness.
  o Focusing on how you can be a safe haven and secure base for the other.
- Sharing your needs and fears clearly and vulnerably with your partner is the antidote to disconnection.

Notes

1. Bowlby, J. (1969/1982). *Attachment and loss: Volume 1 attachment*. New York, NY: Basic Books.
2. Shaver, P. R., & Mikulincer, M. (2016). *Attachment in adulthood: Structure, dynamics and change* (2nd ed.). New York: The Guilford Press.
3. Tennov, D. (1979, 1999). *Love and limerence: The experience of being in love*. Lanham, NY: Scarborough.
4. Bowlby, J. (1979). *The making and breaking of affectional bonds*. London: Tavistock.
5. Tronick, E. Z., & Gianino, A. (1986). Interactive mismatch and repair: Challenges to the coping infant. *Zero to Three*, 6(3): 1–6.

Index

169

Made in the USA
Monee, IL
30 August 2022

12891326R00103